AF651469

ENCYCLOPAEDIA OF EMINENT THINKERS

VOLUME-VIII: **VIVEKANANDA**

Encyclopaedia of Eminent Thinkers Series

Vol. I. The Political Thought of **Mahatma Gandhi**
Vol. II. The Political Thought of **Nehru**
Vol. III. The Political Thought of **Rabindra Nath Tagore**
Vol. IV. The Political Thought of **Radhakrishnan**
Vol. V. The Political Thought of **Vinoba**
Vol. VI. The Political Thought of **Aurobindo**
Vol. VII. The Political Thought of **Jayaprakash Narayan**
Vol. VIII. The Political Thought of **Vivekananda**
Vol. IX. The Political Thought of **Ambedkar**
Vol. X. The Political Thought of **M.N. Roy**

About the Author

K.S. Bharathi did his Master's Degree in Gandhian Thought, Peace-Science, Economics, and Political Science. He also did Postgraduate Diplomas in Politics, Public Administration, Population Dynamics, Gandhian Thought, Tourism, and Telgu. He has contributed some articles in learned journals. He is the author of : *Foundation of Gandhian Thought, Gandhi and Humanity, Socio-Religious Thoughts of Mahatma Gandhi, The Philosophy of Sarvodya, The Satyagraha of Mahatma Gandhi, Gandhi and Nehru, Foundations of Ambedkar Thought, The Social Philosophy of Mahatma Gandhi, Gandhi and Vinoba, The Philosophical Foundations of Gandhian Thought, The Political Thought of Gandhi, The Economic Thought of Gandhi, The Social Thought of Gandhi,* and *The Quintessence and Chronology of Gandhi*. At present, he is the Head of the Postgraduate Department of Gandhian Thought of Nagpur University. He is the Chairman of the Board of Studies of Gandhian Thought, member of the Academic Council, member of the Faculty of Social Sciences, member of the Board of Examination, and member of the Doctoral Research Committee of Nagpur University.

ENCYCLOPAEDIA OF EMINENT THINKERS SERIES-8

VOLUME-EIGHT

THE POLITICAL THOUGHT OF VIVEKANANDA

K.S. BHARATHI
Head, P.G. Dept. of Gandhian Thought,
Nagpur University, Nagpur

CONCEPT PUBLISHING COMPANY, NEW DELHI - 110059

All rights reserved. No part of this work may be reproduced, stored in a retrieval system, or transmitted in any form or by any means, electronic, mechanical, photocopying, microfilming, recording or otherwise, without the prior written permission of the copyright owner and the Publisher.

ISBN 81-7022-709-7 (Vol. 8)
ISBN 81-7022-684-8 (Series)

First Published 1998

© K.S. **Bharathi** (*b.* 1956)

Published and Printed by

Ashok Kumar Mittal
Concept Publishing Company
A/15-16, Commercial Block, Mohan Garden,
NEW DELHI - 110059 (India)

Phones: 5649024, 5648039
Fax 091-011-5648053

TO

MY WIFE

K.B. PUNITHA

PREFACE

There are many valuable books on Vivekananda. There is hardly any book attempting a comprehensive exposition and evaluation of the political thought of Vivekananda. This work seeks to provide a comprehensive exposition of the Political Thought of Vivekananda in a precise and lucid manner.

Vivekananda was a many-sided personality, or rather a many-sided genius. He was a great nationalist of India, who wanted to revitalise the nation through the vitality of religion. He never claimed to be a philosopher or a social reformer in the traditional sense of the term. He was, infact, only a religious man. He thought that if religion is interpreted in its correct sense and understood by everybody, much of our miseries, mutual conflicts and social evils would be automatically solved.

Vivekananda assumed the role of a world teacher and tried to infuse into mankind the essence of unity. He belonged to the whole world and asked. Indians to learn from the West their great concern for masses, reverence and freedom for women and the capacity for making rapid progress. He was a true democrat. He was of the opinion that no nation could gain physical freedom without physical equality. His views on society and its growth were based on his belief that man was not a mere machine, but something more—a divine being. His views on society were humanistic. His humanism was based on his tremendous faith in the powers of man.

I would like to place on record my indebtedness to scholars and thinkers whose ideas enabled me to bring out this book. I gratefully acknowledge the scholars from whose works I have drawn citations viz. Dr. R.C. Gupta, Dr. Bali, Dr. S.L. Mukherjee, Dr. V.D. Mahajan and Swami Vivekananda.

So far as the writing of this book is concerned, whatever success I have achieved is due to the relentless efforts and encouragement of my friend, philosopher and guide, Dr. P.S.G. Kumar, Head, Department of Library and Information Science, Nagpur University. I sincerely express my gratitude to him.

I am indebted to Mr. Ashok Kumar Mittal, Concept Publishing Company for publishing this book in such a short span of time. Finally I hold myself to blame for the errors and shortcomings if any. This work would have not been completed without the grace of Lord Venkateswara of Tirumala and Alamelu Thayar of Tiruchanur.

K.S. BHARATHI

CONTENTS

1

LIFE AND WORK OF VIVEKANANDA

Vivekananda did not seem to belong to this world but appeared to be a radiant being descended from another and higher sphere for a definite purpose. He was a seer, an illuminated soul, very much different from the ordinary run of mankind. His mind was luminous; he had that supreme knowledge of which the *Gita* speaks and which results from the realisation of oneness with the Supreme Being. Besides, he had within himself a fountain of energy to carry his message not only to the different parts of India but to the west also. He never prepared his speeches and addresses, but poured forth the deepest spiritual truths in words of imperishable beauty. Once Sri Ramakrishna said about his young disciple, Narendra, who is known to the world as Swami Vivekananda: "He is not a pond, he is a reservoir. He is not a pitcher or a jug, he is a veritable barrel. He is not a minnow or sardine, he is a huge red-eyed carp. He is not an ordinary sixteen petalled lotus, he is a glorious lotus with a thousand petals".

This beautiful summing up of Vivekananda's personality suggests about his strength, vigour and endurance. A strong athlete, a Herculean figure having broad face spotted with large eyes and vast forehead, he bore in himself a storehouse of power and strength, granite faith and rock of self-confidence, immeasurable passion of a warrior and the Napoleonic ambition for a world conquest. At the same time, he possessed a burning desire for *renunciation* of all earthly empires and for casting off all his chains and roaming like a wandering unknown pilgrim, sheltering under a tree or meditating alone in a lonely cave in the Himalayas.

If one can speak out and signify the life and mission of Swami Vivekananda, the patriot and prophet of modern India, it is strength. A lion among men he roared and thundered forth rousing the leviathan of the sleeping nation from century-old slumber and mental stupor, to rise on its feet and march on freely. He wanted in us the sleeping divinity to awaken that austere elevation of spirit which rouses heroism. He founded the essence of the *Upanishads* and religious scriptures in one word 'manliness'. It was due to his message of courage and fearlessness that he was described as a 'tamer of souls'.

In the words of Jawaharlal Nehru, "Rooted in the past and full of pride in India's heritage, Vivekananda was yet modern in his approach to India's problems and was a kind of bridge between the past of India and her present. He wanted to combine western progress with India's spiritual background". Due to his heroic mood and sometimes even domineering character, Romain Rolland called him 'The Hindu Napoleon'. Vivekananda was not merely an idealist dreamer. He insisted on character-building, discipline and strength of mind. To him, *love* for the Motherland was the first commandment and religion came next. His message to the youth of India was: "Be strong and be fearless". Again, "Above all, be strong, be manly. I have respect even for one who is wicked so long as he is manly and strong, for his strength will make him some day give up his wickedness or even give up all work for selfish ends and will then eventually bring him into the truth". If Rammohan Roy can be called the intellectual progenitor of the liberals, Vivekananda was the spiritual progenitor of the Radicals. Several concepts later on developed by the radical leaders are found in the writings of Vivekananda.

Vivekananda was born as the sixth child of Sri Vishwanath Datta, an extremely popular rich lawyer of Calcutta and his wife Bhuwaneshwari Devi. After a short lived infant son and four daughters, the anxious mother, who was a devotee of Lord Shiva, took special vows and prayed with great sincerity for a son and when she was blessed with one, she truly believed it to be in direct answer to her prayers. In addition, she also had the beautiful dream before his birth in which she saw Shiva getting up from his meditative pose and taking the form of a male child who was to be her son. Thus, her Naren, as Swamiji was called in his childhood, was for her, Lord Shiva Himself.

Swamiji was born on the very auspicious day of Makarsankaranti which the whole country celebrates in a variety of ways. In Bengal, people rush to the Ganges to worship her. According to the English calendar, the day was 12th January 1863. The time was six minutes before Sunrise and his star was *Hasta*. The child was called by his parents as Narendranath but to his family members he was always Biley and to his friends, Naren. Like all great men destined to leave their imprints in the pages of History, Naren early life was also marked with incidents which were pointers to his future greatmen. He surpassed a normal child in his intelligence, courage, fearlessness and total uncontrollable nature earned him the epithet of a naughty child, whom even two nurses or his own mother could hardly control.

Naren's mother would also admonish him saying that if he did not behave properly Lord Shiva would not accept him, nor take him to Kailas. However Naren was assuredly the pride of the family. He was vigorous and active. His sparkling, handsome face winsome manners charmed everybody. Despite his apparent recklessness, exuberance and vigour, he was also capable of being extremely kind hearted and considerate when the situation demanded. To the pet which his father kept at home he was extra kind. Vishwanath Datta had a veritable collection of domestic pets which included cows, horses, goats, peacocks, parrots and gunea pigs. Naren loved him too. A strange reciprocal love existed between them. Cows were his favourites which he often garlanded and decorated.

To attend on *Sanyasins* and other mendicants was a passion with Naren. This joy knew no bounds when a *sanyasi* visited his house. He would spare no effort to see to their comforts and would go on endlessly conversing with them. In addition, he had a strange way of presenting them with whatever was available with him. He could never see anyone going away any such person came to their house. But that could not stop Naren. He would throw through the window whatever was available within his reach to the poor people standing below. His deep love and sympathy for the poor and downtrodden, paved the way to the intensely humanistic approach to life and its problems, which he displayed in his later life.

The *Ramayana* and the *Mahabharata* were his favourites and Sita and Ram were the most worshipful. Soon enough, he installed their images in his prayer room and started worshipping them in his own way. Even from his childhood, Naren evinced great interest in meditation and soon concentration and meditation became his pastime. His tremendous power to meditate and concentrate baffled his friends and parents, as he was often seen sitting in front of his favourite idols, lost to the external world.

Himself physically strong, Naren had a special liking and admiration for strength everywhere and in every form. Among those he admired most in his *childhood* was his father's coachman. Naren loved this coachman with his big moustache and turban, majestically going round with a driving whip in his hand for in him he found his idea of strength and power. One of his childhood ambitions was to become a coachman and he used to proclaim proudly the same. Yes, coach drive he did become but in a different sense. As Swami Vivekananda, he did drive the Nation's coach out of its ruts and started it rolling along a bright new path to glorious destiny.

The coachman was his friend, philosopher and guide. He was often found engaged in serious conversation with the coachman and his opinion was of great importance to Naren. One day in the course of his talk, the coachman told Naren that it was not good to marry. He narrated his own personal experience of married life which was not at all happy and peaceful. Naren was convinced that a married man had to forfeit his freedom and happiness and only misery was his lot. Naren listened to this and immediately decided not to marry. Unfortunately, in his mind, there arose a small contradiction as his favourite deities Rama and Sita, were married. This worried him and upset him so much that he began to weep later, when he confirmed in his mother about this, she told him that he could turn his devotion to Shiva in place of Ram. That very evening he removed the image of Rama and Sita and installed Lord Shiva and started worshipping him. His decision to remain unmarried was irrevocable and he remained a true *Brahmachari* throughout his life.

Naren was a born leader. In his childhood, during his student life and also in his monastic days he always remained the leader of his group. No wonder Sri Ramakrishna, his spiritual *Guru*, ordained him to be the future leader of his *Sanyasin* disciple. In addition to the inborn qualities of leadership of mind and heart he was physically endowed with the dignity and grandeur of a royal personality. People spontaneously looked upto him and accepted him as their leader with a natural ease and confidence, he could exert his will and win over his associates. People felt secure and safe under his leadership and trusted him implicitly. His clarity of thought in planning, his meticulous execution of plans which were so evident in his later life were reflected even in the games he played in childhood.

Physically full of life and vigour, mentally alert and captivating, morally upright and truthful, Naren grew from childhood to youth. He was endowed with a powerful memory and could get by heart long passages with utter ease, greatly impressing his teachers and classmates. There were occasions when for all practical purposes he would appear in attentive, chatting with his friends when the class was on. Teachers would then pull them up but Naren was always ready with quick satisfactory answers, much to the amazement of the teacher. Naren, though he was able to answer the teachers all the same realised that he was an offender and insisted on sharing the punishment with his friends. His ability to answer the questions came out of his rare capacity to do two things at a time talking to his friend's and listening to the teachers simultaneously. He felt that his sense of honour as a pupil would be hurt, if he did not undergo the punishment along with his friends.

Narendra's sense of uprightness was coupled with his awareness to injustice. Once he was subjected to a corporal punishment by a teacher. The teacher was rebuking a boy who, instead of feeling sorry, started laughing which made Naren and his friends also break into laughter. At this the teacher got infuriated and turned to Naren and punished him too, by boxing his ears violently. The ear began to bleed. Naren protested against such punishment. The matter came to the notice of Pandit Ishwar Chandra Vidyasagar who had come to the school. He admonished the teacher and consoled Naren and sent him home. At home, his worried mother pressed him to keep away from school but he attended school the very next day as though nothing had happened. Never in his life did he fear any illwill even towards his worst offenders a noble trait which truly marked his genius.

In those days caste differences were very rigid and certain norms were strictly adhered to. This was something which often baffled Naren. For example, he could not find any rhyme or reason why in his father's parlour were kept different tobacco *hookahs* for clients belonging to different castes. He wanted to find the answer to it in his own way. He wondered what would happen if a *Brahmin* smoked the *hookah* reserved for a Muslim or vice-versa. The explanation which the elders had given was that one would lose one's caste. So, one day, when his father was busy speaking to the clients in another room, Naren decided to test the validity of this statement by smoking from every *hookah*, available in the room. He wanted to see whether that action would lead to any change in his personality. At that juncture his father entered the room and finding Naren near the *hookahs* enquired what he was doing. Naren calmly told him that he was merely trying to see if anything would happen if he violated caste rules. He was convinced that nothing of that sort actually happens.

From his childhood, Naren was more at home in the realm of the soul than of body and mind, once he was escorting his mother and sister to Raipur in the Central Province. He was only 14 years old then. They had to travel a long distance by bullock cart through a dense forest. The lofty mountains on either side of the road, the green vegetation and creepers laden with beautiful coloured flowers, and the sweet chirping of birds of different size, shape and colour thrilled his heart. Suddenly his eyes fell on a bee-hive hanging on one side of huge cliff. All this enchanting beauty of Nature created a deep impression on his mind. The grandeur of nature and the power of destiny absorbed his mind and he passed into an inward bliss, losing all outward consciousness for a considerably long time, during the journey.

Courage coupled with presence of mind, was a unique characteristic of Naren. In an emergency when other would lose their presence of mind and become bewildered, Naren would maintain his poise and act in a surprisingly efficient way, much to the admiration of the people around. There are several instances in his life, where this rare capacity could rescue people from danger.

At college, Naren was in the forefront and had many distinctions to his credit. He was an ardent student of History and Literature. Originally, he was prejudiced against English but later overcame it and became a master in the use of this language. Logic and philosophy were his favourite subjects. He acquainted himself with the science of Modern Medicine. Among the English poets Wordsworth appealed to him most. He was very proficient in making toy machines and engines and had a high mechanical skill. His natural inborn nobility and integrity of character marked him out from his college mates. Though he was humble and modest, he could instinctively sense bad people and scrupulously avoided their company. He was never inclined to untruth of any kind. His thirst for knowledge was phenomenal. Mere learning without deeper realisation, he found insipid. His Principal, Mr. Hastie, is reported to have said, "Naren is really a genius and he would make his mark in life. He had extraordinary intelligence, out of proportion to his physical age."

Though Naren studied many books at great speed and acquired a vast storage of information, he was not directed elsewhere book knowledge. His quest was directed elsewhere. He was western in his heart for which no book had a remedy. He became a member of the *Brahmo Samaj*, the Hindu Reformist Organisation founded by Raja Ram Mohun Roy. Not satisfied with all the theories and beliefs he had read and accumulated, he desired to come face to face with reality. This thirst to experience. Reality dominated his life. It could not be quenched through the knowledge he acquired from the *Brahmo Samaj*. Like a lotus piling for the first rays of the morning sun, Naren too, with his unquenching thirst for the realisation of the ultimate truth, appeared to be waiting for the grace of a true master.

Once it so happened that Mr. William Hastie was teaching English poetry to Naren's class. The topic under discussion was Wordsworth's famous poem *Excursion*. In the poem the poet speaks at length about blissful 'trance' cited the living example of Sri Ramakrishna of Dakshineswar temple as that of a person very frequently experiencing trance and added that this student could go and see him themselves. This roused an interest in Naren, also to meet Sri Ramakrishna.

Narendra was already eagar to meet a man who has had direct experience of the higher kind. In his very first meeting he asked Sri Ramakrishna point blank whether he had seen God, as it was his habit of putting this question to every great man he met. So far none could give him a positive reply of having seen God. But on this occasion, for the first time, he received an answer in the affirmative. Sri Ramakrishna told him that he saw God as clearly as he saw him. He further added that anyone could see and talk to him but people worrying over useless things in life hardly ever took the trouble to see God. This made a deep impression on Naren. He was enchanted by the man who asserted to have seen God.

Sri Ramakrishna was simple, very ordinary looking *Brahman* who was residing as a priest in the Kali Temple, Dakshineswar. At first sight, there was nothing remarkable about him. Therefore, the sophisticated Naren's surrender to Sri Ramakrishna was not immediate as he could not bring himself to believe so easily in the Godliness which was emanating from Sri Ramakrishna. He came away from Dakshineshwar with apparently no further interest in going there again, yet something in his mind carved for the sight of Sri Ramakrishna and at last he submitted to himself to this inner urge.

Aware of Naren's nature of testing before accepting Sri Ramakrishna decided to give him the taste of some spiritual experiences. As days went by Naren felt himself engulfed in an inexplicable feeling of love and intimate comradeship emanating from Sri Ramakrishna. The depth of intimacy that developed between the master and the disciple was truly par excellence and profound beyond description. It did not appear all of a sudden but it grew slowly and steadily. It was one of the holiest of human relationships. The intellect in Naren would not submit easily to the simple religious, spiritual administration of Sri Ramakrishna. In the early days of his discipleship he suffered very much pierced by doubts and disbeliefs.

Reality, in its full scope and glory, Naren's parents were eagar to get him married. But his young mind was already set upon a monastic life of renunciation and service away from earthly pursuits for wealth and power. At one time he even became indifferent to his studies at college. This made his relatives advise him not to meet this strange saint of Dakshineshwar.

In 1884 Naren's father passed away suddenly though he had an excellent practice as a leading lawyer and was earning a lot of money, he was also in the habit of spending it generously on friends, relatives and dependents. As he was the only earning member of the family, on his passing away, the family suddenly fell from its height of affluence into the depths of privation. Even before the period of mourning was over Naren found himself wandering about in the streets of Calcutta in search of a job. Bare-footed, starving, ill-clad, he wandered from office to office under the scorching sun, day after day, seeking a job but without success.

On the one hand Sri Ramakrishna was training him to climb the height of spirituality and on the other hand life adversities were teaching him how to face life and withstand suffering. The experience of these eventful years stood him in good stand in his monastic life and added to his indomitable will and courage.

Many were the days on which Naren would be starving yet, unable to bear the pitiable condition of his people at home, he would tell his mother that he had already eaten elsewhere so that the little food available at home might be shared by others. The months of acute physical hunger and suffering contributed much to the building up of special strength in Naren's personality. In later years, as a champion of the cause of the poor when he spoke, he did so from the depth of his heart, out of his own first hand experience of hunger, thirst, neglect and indifference at the hands of society. His heart forever strongly and touchingly throbbed in unison with the poor and underprivileged.

This teacher-disciple relationship lasted only for five years. In respect of time, they were just years, but in fact in respect of their significance, they were truly years. They were the years when young Naren was getting trained and transformed to carry on the great work that he was to do in his later years slowly and steadily. Sri Ramakrishna took him through all the steps in spiritual unfoldment in addition to teaching him all the important lessons which formed part of his unique message the most significant of which was, that no one should show mere condescension to another human being. The right attitude was to worship and adore the human being as part of the Divine.

On 16 August, 1886, Sri Ramakrishna entered into *Mahasamadhi*. But before that event, he had transferred his entire spiritual power to him thus endowing him with an immense spiritual strength and had appointed Naren as his successor to lead the group of disciples.

After setting his brother disciples, he began his life of *Parivrajata*—wandering monk and travelled through the length and breadth of the country. He mixed freely with princes and paupers alike and came to perceive at first hand, indigenous strength and weakness and the problems facing our country and her people. On one side, he saw the unparallelled glorious cultural heritage of the past and on the other the abject poverty and ignorance of the masses, both in body and mind. This disturbed him terribly. The cultural crisis which India was passing through clearly appeared before his vision. The total breakdown of the political power had shaken the people faith in the potency of her age old philosophy. Ignorance and neglect of our religion and philosophy were creating conflicts in their mind, destroying their simple inherent faith and leading to a peculiar slavishness in mentality.

During his wandering, one fact stood out before him. That was his own conviction and firm resolution to carry out fully and unconditionally his Masters Commands and dedicate the rest of his life to the service of his fellowmen. To his brother disciples at Baranagore he said, "I have now travelled all over India but alas, it was agony to me, my brothers to see with my own eyes the terrible poverty, and misery of the masses and I could not restrain my tears. It is now my firm conviction that it is futile to preach religion among them without first trying to remove their poverty and sufferings". During his travels he had occasions to live with the outcastes and untouchables. He was deeply moved by their misery and enforced degradation. Their silent submission to all the religious and social injustices pained his heart very deeply.

On 24 December, 1892, Vivekananda reached the southernmost tip of India, Kanyakumari. He swam the ocean and reached to a rock and sat. Here he got the knowledge, the *jyana*, of God. He revealed and was convinced that his service to the God must begin with the service to humanity of India. He exclaimed, "May I be born again and again and suffer a thousand miseries, if only I may worship the only God in whom I believe, the sum total of all souls, and above all, my God the wicked, my God the afflicted, my God the poor of all races".

In this tour itself an idea of attending meeting, 'Parliament of Religion' to be held at Chicago in U.S.A. in September 1893 came. Initially he was confused about going. But finally he decided to attend this meeting as a representative of India. Vivekananda considered America as a country of unlimited opportunities, where people's mind were free from the encumberance of castes or classes. His mission in going to America was thus to give receptive Americans the ancient wisdom of India and bring back to his motherland, the knowledge of science and technology. Apart from enhancing India's prestige in the Occident, he wanted to create a new confidence among his own people.

Vivekananda got the invitation for this Parliament of Religion on 3 August, 1890. He got huge and unexpected donations for this journey. On 31 May, 1893, he started his voyage from Bombay by ship. He reached Chicago, via Vancouver, on 25 July, 1893. He was very early for the conference. Professor Wright encouraged him to represent *Hinduism* in the Parliament of Religion. He wrote about him to the chairman of the committee on the selection of delegates, thus, "Here is a man more learned than all our learned professors put together".

The Parliament started on 11 September, 1893 at 10 a.m. In numerical order Vivekananda's position was number thirty-one, when his turn came he addressed the audience as 'Sisters and Brothers of America'. Instantly, thousands arose in their seats and gave him loud applause which lasted for full two minutes. He conquered this Parliament and became world famous personality instantly.

The Conference came to an end on 24 September, 1893. Vivekananda's lectures appealed to the intellectuals of

America so much so that people were ready to wait for his lecture to any extent. At this time his name was 'Swami Vivekananda' which then became his name for the rest of his life.

After this Conference Swamiji toured all over America delivering lectures on propagation of Hindu Dharma. While he was touring, he not only delivered the lectures but studied American life in various aspects, especially the secrets of country's high standard of living. Through his lectures he also earned money which he utilised for himself, and for his philanthropic and religious projects in India. But the important thing that he wanted to achieve through these lectures was to broadcast his ideas all over American continent and thus to remove erroneous notions regarding Hindu religion and society from people's mind. Through his lectures he became 'Cyclonic Hindu' for western people. He established Vedantic Society in 1894.

After two years in America in mid of 1895, Swami Vivekananda took rest. It was mainly to restore his health. He stayed at Thousand Island Park where he started classes to manufacture 'Few *Yogis*'. Starting with the Gospel according to Saint John, from *Bible*, for his Christian students, he taught them from *Gita*, the *Upanishads*, the *Vedanta Sutras*, the *Bhakti Sutras* of Narda and other Hindu scriptures. He always stressed morality as the basis of the spiritual life. To him there could be no spirituality without truth, non-injury, continence, non-stealing, cleanliness and austerity.

After this Swami Vivekananda visited Europe for about two months. He was very eager to test his ability as an interpreter of spiritual culture of India in the very citadel of English speaking nation and to a nation which ruled India for more than one hundred and forty years by that time. He very successfully conveyed his mission. He praised the capacity of Englishmen to talk less and work more. During this stay he got his greatest disciple Miss Margarette Noble who eventually became Sister Nivedita.

Swami Vivekananda once again came to New York on 6

December, 1895. After this, he again toured different places in America. In 1896, the *Vedanta Society* became better organised. Its motto was tolerance and religious universalism. He was offered the chair of Eastern Philosophy in Harward University in March 1896. Similar offer was made by Columbia University. He declined both the offers on the ground that he was a *Sanyasin*. During this period, he translated many Hindu thoughts into western languages.

Swami Vivekananda started his journey back to India in 1897. He reached Colombo on 15 January. On 20 January, he reached Calcutta via Madras. He was feted there by huge crowd which was waiting for this great son of India.

On 1 May, 1897, Ramakrishna Mission Association came into existence. The aims and methods of actions were true to the spirit of Swami Vivekananda, namely: (a) to train the men so as to make them competent to teach such knowledge and science as are conducive to the material and spiritual welfare of the masses; (b) to promote and encourage arts and industries; (c) to introduce and spread among the people in general Vedantic and other ideas as elucidated in the life of Sri Ramakrishna. These aims and ideas of Ramakrishna Mission Association are purely spiritual and humanitarian and had no connection with politics. Swami Vivekananda was the General President of the Association.

From May 1897, Swami Vivekananda toured and lectured extensively in Northern India, Uttar Pradesh, Punjab, Kashmir. He sowed seeds of rejuvenated Hinduism everywhere. In the early part of 1898 site for Belur Math was purchased. On 9 December, 1899, the Ramakrishna Monastry at Belur was formally consecrated. He set the working of his disciple in India.

On 20 June, 1899, Swami Vivekananda undertook his second tour to America. During this tour he delivered more than 90 lectures. He also reviewed the progress of the work he started during his first visit. He returned to India via Paris, Vienna, Athens and Mistra on 9 December, 1900.

Continuous touring and lecturing deteriorated the health of Swami Vivekananda. Moreover, he himself felt that the mission he started could continue. He wanted that his disciples should shoulder the responsibility of the mission assigned to him by his master, Sri Ramakrishna. Accordingly, he started distributing his works among his disciples. After registration of Deed of Belur Math on 2 February, 1901, he started this distribution from Mayawati Ashram. He left chairmanship of Ramakrishna Mission Association to Swami Brahmananda, and appointed Swami Suradananda as secretary.

Swami Vivekananda, as had definite ideas about life, had the same for his death. He had selected the site of his cremation. He never wanted to live more than forty years. It thus can very well be said that the end did not come to him but he brought the end to him on 4 July, 1902, at 9.10 p.m. At the time of his death, rather *Mahasamadhi*, his age was 39 years, 5 months and 24 days.

Swami Vivekananda born on the East Coast of India and breathed his last at Belur Math on the bank of sacred river Ganga. He is pride not only of India but of whole world. Even today, and time and again his name, and works give inspiration to thousands of youths.

2

INFLUENCES ON VIVEKANANDA

Vishwanath Dutta

An attorney at law of the High Court of Calcutta Vishwanath Dutta was a cultured man of his time. His life was influenced by western as well as Islamic style apart from his Bengali family background. He was well versed in English and Persian literature. To him, *Bible* and poetry of Hafiz contained truths unmatched elsewhere. Through his strict vigilance Vishwanath Dutta gave lessons of discipline to child Narendra. He taught him good manners the deviation from which his father would never tolerate.

The great quality which his father gave him was generosity of heart and sympathetic view to poor and deprived ones. He always helped his poor relatives financially, some of whom were habituated of drinking. Narendra protested against this. And his father gave him reality of life in very appropriate works: "How can you understand the great misery of human life? When you will realise the depths of human suffering you will sympathise with these unfortunate creatures who try to forget their sorrows, even though only for a short while, in the oblivion created by intoxicants".

His father gave child Narendra a great advice when he asked his father, "How shall I conduct myself in the world". His father replied, "Never show surprise of anything". This advice enabled Vivekananda to live equally among princes and pariah maintaining his serenity.

The qualities of courage, straight-forwardness and broad mindedness was gift of his father. His father gave him regard for truth whenever found, and his sceptical attitude towards the religious beliefs and social conventions of the Hindu society of that time.

Bhuvaneshwari Devi

Bhuvaneshwari Devi belonged to the old tradition of Hindu womanhood. She was very religious. Since childhood, she made good '*sanskara*' on Narendra. Narendra was influenced very much by her qualities of special refuge of the poor, calm resignation to God, inner tranquillity and dignified detachment. Through her mode of living she taught little Narendra great values of truth, purity, respect for others while maintaining self respect and strong will and calmness.

On one occasion when Narendra was unjustly treated at school, his mother gave him consolation. She said, "My child, what does it matter, if you are right? Always follow the truth without caring about the result. Very often you may have to suffer injustice or unpleasant consequences for holding to the truth, but you must not under any circumstances abandon it". Apart from telling him stories from *Ramayana* and *Mahabharata* she gave him early education. She taught him Bengali alphabet and his first English words.

Mother Bhuvaneshwari Devi played vital role in bringing out innate virtues. His mother was stipped in the spiritual heritage of India. Vivekananda's habit of thinking highly, acting nobly and of discipline were acquired from his mother. Many years later, he acknowledged this to his audience. He said, "I am indebted to my mother for whatever knowledge I have acquired".

Durga Prasad

Durga Prasad, grandfather of Vivekananda, left family to lead monastic life when his son Vishwanath Dutta was a child. Narendra had special fancy for wandering monks, a quality certainly inherited by him from his grandfather. Narendra always offered anything he could give as alms to the monks. One day he offered his only possession a tiny piece of new clothes that was wrapped round his waist. Since childhood, it seems, Narendra had decided to become *sanyasin*.

Brajendra Nath

Brajendra Nath was the college friend of Narendra, who later became leading Indian philosopher of his time. Narendra studied poet Shelley under Brajendra Nath. He tried to present Narendra with synthesis of the supreme Brahman of Vedanta, the Universal Reason of Hegel, and the Gospel of Liberty, Equality and Fraternity of the French revolution. By this Narendra could achieve an intellectual victory, scepticism and materialism.

Brajendra Nath was platonic transcendentalist and did not have faith in artificial prop of grace, or the mediation of a *guru*. He told Narendra only to rely upon Pure Reason and to identify self with it to experience an ineffable peace. Though he could not satisfy Narendra's urge for peace of mind he definitely influenced his reasoning.

Prof. William Hastie

Prof. William Hastie was the Principal of General Assembly College, Calcutta. He used to teach philosophy to Narendra and his friends. He encouraged discussions on various subjects. Narendra was his favourite student regarding whom he said, "Narendra is a real genius, I have travelled far and wide, but have not yet come across a lad of his talents and possibilities even among the philosophical students in German Universities. He is bound to make his mark in life".

William Hastie had high regards for Sri Ramakrishna Paramhansa. He regarded trances of Ramakrishna

Paramhansa as result of purity and concentration. In his disturbed state of mind regarding existence of God and in his craze to see God face to face Narendra remembered Prof. William Hastie's remark on Ramakrishna: "I have known only one person who has realised that blessed state, and he is Ramakrishna of Dakshineshwar. You will understand trances if you visit the saint".

Western Influence

Vivekananda was a person of intellect. He never accepted anything, even views and advise of Sri Ramakrishna Paramhansa, till he was satisfied of its scientific angle. Moreover his father's life style and the schools and colleges where he took education were bound to influence him. He had great respect for analytical scientific methods. He had taken course in western medicines to understand the functioning of the nervous system, particularly brain and spinal cord, in order to find out secrets of Sri Ramakrishna's trances.

Vivekananda studied English poets, Wordsworth and Shelley. Their poems stirred his feelings. He deeply felt with Shelley his pantheism, impersonal love and vision of a glorified millennial humanity. His study of John Stuart Mill's *Three Essays on Religion* upset his boyish theism and easy optimism imbibed from *Brahmo Samaj*. He studied Hume's scepticism and Herbert Spencer's Doctrine of Unknowable. These studies filled his mind with a settled philosophical agnoticism.

All the western influences developed matter-of-fact vision in Narendra. On one hand he searched for truth in day to day life, but on the other hand he was more and more confused. His study of human nature on western line increased his inner turmoil. He could not stand with the view that universe is a mere lifeless, loveless mechanism. Whereas initial western influences led him to some confusions, by the time he met Max Muller in Oxford on 28

May, 1896, he had become disciple of Sri Ramakrishna.

Max Muller, the great German Sanskritist, and Indologist had great love for India. He was greatly influenced by the spirituality of Sri Ramakrishna and had already published an article on Sri Ramakrishna in 'Nineteenth Century', entitled 'A Real Mahatma'.

Brahmo Samaj

The Brahmo Samaj was the prominent liberal movement founded by Raja Ram Mohun Roy. The introduction of English education had given new views of life to the youths. It also brought into focus many drawbacks of society. Brahmo Samaj was foremost to realise the importance of the western rational method for solving the diverse problems of Hindu society.

The youths at that time had very natural tendency to get attracted to this movement, Narendra also felt the appeal of its progressive ideas and became one of its members. Brahmo Samaj movement influenced him in formative period of his life.

As a member of Brahmo Samaj, Narendra accepted its doctrine of monotheism and the personal God. He regarded doctrine of non-dualistic Vedanta i.e. divinity of soul and oneness of existence as blasphemy. As a loyal member of Brahmo Samaj he was critical of image worship and the rituals of Hindu religion. But Narendra had in him deep roots of purity and spirituality. Brahmo Samaj could not satisfy this deep yearning of spirituality. The congregational prayers and devotional songs of Brahmo Samaj, though exhilarated his mind, could not give him any real experience.

Prominent leaders of Brahmo Samaj after Raja Ram Mohun Roy were Devendra Nath Tagore, a great devotee of *Upanishads* and Keshabchandra Sen inclined to doctrines and rituals of Christianity. Narendra, though influenced by Brahmo Samaj, was not satisfied with intellectual and eclectic approval of Brahmo Samaj. Brahmo Samaj could not satisfy deep yearning of his soul. He wanted to realise God, the goal of religion. He wanted a person who had seen God face to face. Leaders of Brahmo Samaj advised him to practice meditation but could not help in his spiritual struggle.

Scriptures

Since childhood like every Indian boy, Narendra was told stories from *Ramayan, Mahabharat, Vedas* and *Puranas*. It had natural influence on him. He developed love for Hindu deities. He was initially very much influenced by Rama for his heroism and faithful life with Sita. He started worshipping Rama. But as he had no great love for marriage he could not continue to worship Rama-Sita. He replaced their idols with Shiva—the Lord of *Yogis*. But his love for Rama was unending. He was influenced by Hanuman for his strength.

Narendra was greatly influenced by the story of Nachiketa from *Kenopanishad*. It says that if one goes after ultimate truth, the songs, women and gold and rest of it are to be rejected. He had natural instinct to become *Sanyasin*. He also developed self respect from stories of Nachiketa.

Since his student life, Narendra was a voracious reader. He read much of the Indian and foreign literature during this period. His father used to encourage not only reading but discussions with authorities in various subjects. Narendra was also a symbol of strength and courage. He was a very active youth. He wanted all youth to be strong, healthy and manly.

Narendra was also greatly influenced by the *Upanishads*. His spiritual base was established by *Upanishads*. Influence of *Upanishads* was so great that till he finally became the disciple of Ramakrishna and Kali he could not preach Kali in public because he thought that all that modern man required was to be found in the *Upanishads*. He considered *Upanishads* to be shining strength and bright philosophy which proclaim that the greatest truths are the simplest things in the world, simple as your own existence. He considered *Upanishads* to be great mine of strength.

Narendra was also influenced by *Gita*. He considered it to be answer of each and all problems. The concept of Brahman was understood from *Gita*. The importance of *Karma* (duty) is also highlighted in *Gita*. He understood the fact, work is worship from *Gita*.

Christianity

As a student Narendra was greatly influenced by western culture. He had studied *Bible*. Missionary work was in progress during those days. Life of Jesus influenced him greatly. Thus before taking *diksha*—an oath for *Sanyasin* life—he asked his fellow monks to live like Christ who had no place to lay his head. He considered his mission of awakening of India like Cross.

Islam

Since childhood Narendra was in touch with Muslims due to his father's varied social contacts. He had read *Koran* and was very much impressed by its originality, purity and freeness from interpolation since eleven hundred years. The spirit of democracy and equality in Islam appealed him.

Buddha

Since childhood Narendra was influenced by Gautam Buddha. It was mainly for the reason that Buddha left all contacts and became *Sanyasin*. In his childhood when he used to try meditate, he used to see an illuminated figure which he thought to be of Buddha. He had special affection for Buddha. He believed that the history of India has been changed by noble teachings of Buddha.

Sri Ramakrishna Paramhansa

Narendranath was in a confused state of mind when he was

with Brahmo Samaj. The rational views of *Brahmo-Samaj* and his spiritual yearning caused great upheavals in the mind of Narendra. He wanted to see God face to face. He contacted many but nobody except Sri Ramakrishna Paramhansa confidently told him about existence of God and promised to show him God.

It is very difficult to say who was influenced by whom among these two—one the master and other the disciple. Sri Ramakrishna behaved during their first visit as if he was waiting for Narendra since long. And Narendra was not ready to believe Sri Ramakrishna under the influence of his western rational mentality. But it was Sri Ramakrishna who had thrown light on *philosophy* of non-dualism with its discipline of non-attachment and on that of dualism with its discipline of love. In his own appealing manner Sri Ramakrishna very successfully turned the vibrant youth who was in confused state of mind to Hindu spiritual philosophy from his western and Brahmo Samaj background. Sri Ramakrishna emphasised that to see world alone, without God is ignorance, *ajnan*, to see God, alone, without world, is a kind of philosophical knowledge *jnana*, but to see all beings permeated by the spirit of God is supreme wisdom, *vijnana*.

Sri Ramakrishna taught Narendra three salient disciplines of Vaishnavism viz. love of God's name, service to the devotees and compassion for all living beings. But he did not like the word compassion. Instead he wanted the service of all considering them to be God's manifestation. In Narendra, Sri Ramakrishna found his heir who could continue his unfinished task. He never wanted Narendra to be after *Mukti* of his own. He understood the potential of Narendra to be very great for *Mukti* of world. Thus when Narendra requested him for a boon of remaining in *Samadhi* three or four days at a stretch Sri Ramakrishna said to Naren: "Shame on you, you are asking for such an insignificant thing. I thought that you would be like a big banyan tree, and that thousands of people would rest in your shade. But now I see you are seeking your own liberation".

It was the teaching of Sri Ramakrishna that developed concept of service to *Daridra-narayan* in Vivekananda. Under his influence only Narendra began to believe that God becomes man so that man may become God.

3

INFLUENCES OF VIVEKANANDA

Vivekananda may truly be called the spiritual father of the Indian regeneration movement in the twentieth century. Romain Rolland said, "The Master's rough scourge made her turn for the first time in her sleep, and for the first time the heroic trumpet sounded in the midst of her dream the Forward March of India, conscious of her God. She never forget it. From that day the awakening of the torpid Colossus began. If the generation that followed, saw, three years after Vivekananda's death, the revolt of Bengal, the prelude to the great movement of Tilak and Gandhi, if India today has definitely taken part in the collective action of organised masses, it is due to the initial shock, to the mighty Lazarus, come forth".[1]

According to Dr. R.C. Majumdar, "Swami Vivekananda gave a spiritual basis to Indian nationalism. The lessons of the *Vedanta* and *Bhagavad Gita* permeated the lives and activities of many nationalists, and many a martyr, inspired by his teachings, endured extreme sufferings and sacrifices with a cheerful heart, fearlessly embraced death, and calmly bore inhuman tortures worse than death, which were sometimes inflicted upon them".[2] The Sedition Committee found that the revolutionaries had deified Vivekananda and their personal effects mainly consisted of the *Gita* and volumes of Swami Vivekananda's works.

Romain Rolland observed, "Curzon's partition plan was a death blow aimed at the brain and the heart of India: for

Bengal was her most keenly alive Province and the one from whose intelligence and attachment to her great past British supremacy had most to fear. Bengal revolted. In a few months the face of the country was changed. Press, gallery, temples, theatre, literature all became national".[3] Vivekananda's inspiration to the nationalist movement can be had from Subhas Chandra's The Indian struggle. "Though the Swami never gave any political message, everyone who came into contact with him or his writings developed a spirit of patriotism and a political mentality. So far as Bengal is concerned, Swami Vivekananda may be regarded as the spiritual father of modern nationalist movement".[4]

According to Dr. R.C. Majumdar, "Militant nationalism was sustained and encouraged by the precepts and examples of such men as Surendra Nath Banerjee, Swami Vivekananda, B.G. Tilak and Rabindranath Tagore, though none of them perhaps directly lent support to it. It has been said of some of these and many other leaders that they had occasionally lent their moral support to the cult of militant nationalism, but it is difficult either to prove or disprove it".[5]

The origin of national unity can largely be attributed to Vivekananda, and because of this he has left a definite stamp on our socio-political history of the period. Mahendranath Datta directly traces the influence of Vivekananda upon Tilak in this connection. The essence of nationality is the feeling of unity among a people and an urge for a concerted action on their part. Vivekananda said, "A common danger, or sometimes a common cause of hatred or love, is the bond that binds people together. By the same law that herds beasts of prey together, men also unite into a body and form a caste or a nation of their own".[6] This feeling of unity, which is the first essential of a nationality and is called nationalism, could not be forged among the different sections of the Indian population in any remarkable degree, because no common bond could be created, nor could any common aspiration be held out before them by any of the movements.

Vivekananda was sure that so long as the Congress remained a debating society of the Westernised section of the population, not much hope could be entertained of it. Without man-making, without associating the people with the organisation and making service its base, certainly not much could be expected of the Indian National Congress. Dr. A.D. Pusalker is of the opinion that the change in the Congress policy and programme was, in no small measure, due to Vivekananda's influence upon the Congressmen of his generation. C.F. Andrews said, "The Swami's intrepid patriotism gave a new colour to the national movement throughout India. More than any other single individual of that period Vivekananda had made his contribution to the new awakening of India. Even without being connected with the Congress, he largely shaped its policy and promoted its evolution."[7]

Another important contribution of Vivekananda to contemporary and subsequent life is to be found in the substitution of devotionalism and feminity, which were largely revived during the Renaissance period by Keshabchandra Sen, by the worship of strength. Vivekananda repeatedly proclaimed that he wanted "muscles of iron and nerves of steel". Nehru said, "Vivekananda spoke of many things but the one constant refrain of his speech and writing was *abhay*—be fearless, be strong. For him man was no miserable sinner but a part of *divinity*; why should he be afraid of anything? If there is sin in the world it is weakness; avoid all weakness, weakness is sin, weakness is death. That had been the great lesson of the *Upanishads*. Fear breeds evil and weeping and wailing. There had been enough of that, enough of softness. What our country wants now are muscles of iron and nerves of steel".[8]

Vivekananda was the first to draw the attention of the leaders of India to the social implication of the poverty of the masses. But none before him had pointed out that *freedom* of the people from want of daily bread was the first condition of national regeneration and social growth. His challenge was for regeneration of the country through the reawakening of the masses. The masses could not be reawakened, if they did not get bare necessities.

Vivekananda's triumph in the West helped considerably in reviving faith of the Indian people in their own things. Bipin Chandra Pal said, "Some people in India think that very little fruit has come of the lectures that Swami Vivekananda delivered in England and his friends and admirers exaggerate his work. But on coming here I see he had exerted a marked influence everywhere. In many parts of England I have met with men who deeply regard and venerate Vivekananda. Though I do not belong to this sect, and though it is true that I have differences of opinion with him, I must say that Vivekananda has opened the eyes of a great many here and broadened their hearts. Owing to his teaching, most people here now believe firmly that wonderful spiritual truths lie hidden in the ancient Hindu scriptures. Not only has he brought about this feeling, but he has succeeded in establishing a golden relation between England and India".[9]

Though Tilak and Vivekananda were working in separate fields, both of them were working at the same time in leavening their respective movements with the national spirit by requisitioning into service the two great forces of nationalism: history and religion. However, Tilak was acting in this regard consciously and in an organised way, while Vivekananda was doing this in his prophet's role. Both were after the restoration of the *Gita's* dynamic doctrine of action for the welfare of the world. Both belonged to different fields, but they ran parallel and each supplemented the other's action. *History* and *religion* came to be associated as one idea in Vivekananda's mind, and Tilak, with whom Vivekananda had many interesting conversations, must have got a glimpse of it.

Vivekananda's influence on Tagore is more clearly discernible. Romain Rolland said, "The present leaders of India; the king of thinkers, the king of poets and the Mahatma—Aurobindo Ghose, Tagore and Gandhi—have grown, flowered and bore fruit under the double constellation of the Swan and the Eagle—a fact publicly acknowledged by Aurobindo and Gandhi. . . As for Tagore, whose Goethe-like genius stands at the junction of all the rivers of India, it is permissible to presume that in him are united and harmonised the two currents of the Brahmo Samaj and of the new Vedantism of Ramakrishna and Vivekananda. Rich in both, free in both, he has serenely wedded the West and the East in his own spirit. . . There is no doubt that the breadth of such a forerunner must have played some part in his evolution".[10]

Tagore had been writing patriotic poems from the beginning of his career, but a few which he composed during the 1905 upheaval bear an undeniable imprint of Vivekananda. The emergence of Tagore as a man of the East and the West, and in this transformation Vivekananda's influence seems to be considerable. Though not fully acknowledging the debt, Tagore pays glowing tribute to Vivekananda as a man of the East and the West coming in the procession of Rammohun, Ranade and Bankimchandra. Tagore said, "The ultimate truth in man is not in his intellect or in his material wealth, it is in his imagination of sympathy, in his illumination of heart, in his activities of self-sacrifice, in his capacity for extending love far and wide across the barriers of caste and colour, in his realising this world not as a store-house of mechanical power but as a habitation of man's soul with its eternal music of beauty and in its inner light of divine presence".[11]

Aurobindo described Vivekananda as a king among men and the leading exemplar and the most powerful exponent of the philosophy of preservation by reconstruction, which is the essence of his philosophy as well. He publicly acknowledged that he was inspired by the vision of Vivekananda during his meditations in prison. To him, Vivekananda is the architect of our national life; he is its chief leader. What was his ideal yesterday has become India's to-day. He said, "Vivekananda was a soul of puissance if ever there was one, a very lion among men. . . . we perceive his influence still working gigantically, we know not well how, we know not well where, in something that is not yet formed, something leonine, grand, intuitive, upheaving, that has entered the soul of India and we say, Behold! Vivekananda still lives in the soul of his Mother and in the souls of her children".[12] To quote Dr. K.R. Srinivasa Iyengar, "He (Aurobindo) had an immense admiration for Vivekananda and a much deeper feeling for Ramakrishna. But he did not altogether accept Vivekananda's philosophy or standpoint".[13]

Aurobindo found in Vivekananda "a nobler and more inspiring patriotism" which he was in search of. He further found in him the endorsement of his belief in the need for 'Purification by Blood and Fire', which can largely be equated with Vivekananda's renunciation and service. Aurobindo remained very much philosophical in his social and political outlook and came to furnish nationalism and kindred ideas with the much needed philosophical base, and in these Vivekananda's influence can be clearly traced.

Gandhiji publicly acknowledged that the reading of Vivekananda's works had increased his patriotism. He said, "I have come here to pay my homage, and respect to the revered memory of Swami Vivekananda whose birth is being celebrated today. I have gone through his words very thoroughly and after having gone through them, the love that I had for my country has become a thousand fold. I ask you, young men, not to go away empty-handed without imbibing something of the spirit of the place where Swami Vivekananda lived and died". Thus he acknowledged that he had gone through Swami Vivekananda's works thoroughly and it had increased his patriotism.

Both in the perception of his mission and in the technique devised Gandhiji had Vivekananda as his forerunner. For example, the element of non-violent non-cooperation in Gandhi's technique may clearly be regarded as largely derived from the philosophy of strength of Vivekananda. Dr. Pusalkar said, "Swamiji's Don't-touchism found an echo in the Harijan movement for the abolition of untouchability. . . . The concept of *Daridra Narayan* also owes its existence to the Swamiji's lead".[14] Vivekananda carried on a crusade against untouchability and a tirade against the priests, but he never wanted to eliminate the Brahmin class. What he wanted was to make them true Brahmins and elevate others to their level and thereby to eliminate the *Shudras* altogether.

REFERENCES

1. *Life of Swami Vivekananda and the Universal Gospel, op. cit.*, pp. 113-14.
2. *Supra*, p. 197.
3. *Prophets, op. cit.*, pp. 497-98.
4. *Supra*, p. 197.
5. *Freedom Movement*, Vol. I, p. 447.
6. *Supra*, p. 471.
7. *Patriot-Saint, op. cit.*, pp. 3-4.
8. *Discovery of India, op. cit.*, p. 282.
9. *Life*, p. 441.
10. *Prophets*, pp. 462-63.
11. *Construction versus Creation* (Lectures and Addresses, p. 76).
12. *Dayananda, Bankim-Tilak-Dayananda, op.cit.*, pp. 41-42.
13. *Sri Aurobindo*, pp. 41-42.
14. *Prophets*, p. 460.

4

VIVEKANANDA—A REVIVALIST OR REFORMER

Vivekananda was both a revivalist and a reformer. He was a revivalist in so far as he tried to revive. Indian traditions and not to imitate the West. He was a reformer in as much as he sought to incorporate the modern spirit of social and economic equality in Indian society. He tried to assimilate the modern rationalistic spirit of the west without discarding Indian spirituality. Although he defended image worship, yet he described it as the lowest form of worship. Although he spoke in favour of social reform, he raised his voice of protest against any attack on Indian institutions merely because the westerners disapproved of the same.

Vivekananda was against the indiscriminate imitation of the western ways of life. According to him, "We must grow according to our nature. Vain is to attempt the lines of action that foreign societies have engrafted upon us: It is impossible. Glory unto God, that it is impossible, that we cannot be twisted and tortured into the shape of other nations. I do not condemn the institutions of other races; they are good for them, but not for us. With other sciences, other institutions and other traditions behind them, they have got their present system. We, with our traditions, with thousands of years of *Karma* behind us, naturally can only follow our own bent, run in our own grooves and that we shall have to do. We cannot become westerns; therefore, imitating the western is useless. Suppose you can imitate the westerns, that moment you will die, you will have no more life in you. A stream is taking its rise, away beyond where time began flowing through millions of ages of human history; do you mean to get hold of that stream, and push it back to its source, to a Himalayan glacier? Even if that were practicable, it would not be possible for you to be Europeanised. If you find it it impossible for the European to throw off the few centuries of old culture which there is in the west, do you think it is possible for you to throw off the culture of shining scores of centuries? It cannot be. To Europeanise India is, therefore, an impossible and foolish task".

Vivekananda wanted to stimulate the pride of Indians in their own customs, civilisation and way of life. He travelled and lectured in every nook and corner of India and spoke against mere imitation and indiscriminate westernisation. He deplored the growing denationalisation of the Indians under the impact of the western culture.

Vivekananda stood for radical reforms in Hindu society but he did not approve of the approach and the language used by the socialist reformers in India. His view was that the social reformers had confined their activities to the upper castes and classes and had not touched the masses at all. They had put greater emphasis on widow remarriage which affected primarily the upper classes than on the removal of untouchability which concerned the masses. He said, "Most of the reforms that have been agitated during the last century have been ornamental. Every one of these reforms only touches the first-two castes. Every effort has been spent in cleaning own houses, making themselves nice and in looking pretty before foreigners. That is no reformation".

Vivekananda called upon the reformers to go to the masses. He was a *Karmayogi* and he drowned himself in ceaseless activity for the uplift of India. In the United States, he was called the 'Cyclonic Hindu'. His death at the age of 39 was a great loss to the world in general and India in particular.

It is true that Vivekananda was a revivalist and a reformer but he also impressed upon his countrymen the urgent need of learning western sciences and coming into intimate contact with foreigners. His view was that one important cause of the degeneration of the Hindus was that believing that they could do without the world, they refused to travel to foreign countries. He called upon the Hindus not to observe those social laws which prohibited them from crossing the seas or going to foreign lands. He himself set the example by visiting the foreign countries many times.

Vivekananda called upon his countrymen to learn the methods of modern sciences and the liberal ideals of social organisation from the west. His view was that in the past though Indians enjoyed freedom in matters of religion, yet because they enjoyed very little freedom in social matters, they developed a cramped and crystallised society. His view was that the Englishmen were the instrument sent by God to break the crystallised society of India. He considered it as one of the benefits of the British rule in India. He believed in the policy of moderation in the field of social reform. His view was that mere denunciation and condemnation create unnecessary social tension and antagonism.

5

ETERNAL VALUES IN VIVEKANANDA

Vivekananda stood for all-round freedom—physical, mental and spiritual as well as social and political. He stood also for eternal norms of life which clearly imply a new form of bondage. Sister Nivedita said, "The truth he preaches would have been as true, had he never been born. Nay more, they would have been equally authentic. The difference would have been in their difficulty of access, in their want of modern clearness and incisiveness of statement and in their loss of mutual coherence and unity. Had he not lived, texts that today will carry the bread of life to thousands might have remained the obscure dispute of scholars. He taught with authority, and not as one of the *Pundits*. For he had plunged to the depths of the realisation which he preached and he came back, like Ramanuja, only to tell its secrets to the pariah, the outcaste and the foreigner".[1]

According to Vivekananda, man is not a puny creature of blood and bones, he is not merely a volitional creature either. In his real nature he is the king of spirit. Since the essence of spirit is growth, the cult of growth becomes the kernel of his philosophy. For him, growth in the context of struggle, is the sign of life—individual, social and national as well as international. Therefore, fulfilment of life implies its fullest development. In his view, man is in bondage. His clarion call is for all-round freedom—physical, mental and spiritual as well as social and political. He fully recognised and propagated the eternal axiom that freedom is the condition of securing growth.

Growth must always be from within and according to one's own law of growth. Vivekananda found the so-called civilised peoples came to boast much about the progress of civilisation. To him, theirs was just a case of making virtue of a necessity. But it was a dangerous practice, since by deceiving others they were also deceiving themselves. Freedom is also necessary to perceive harmony with all other human beings. When one perceives harmony with all human beings, one cannot have any desire to hold others in bondage—social or political. Perception of unity presupposes perception of equality with all members of the species, and this cannot be possible without freedom.

Vivekananda seeks to realise fraternity not by asserting rights but by inculcating in the individual a sense of duty and part of his very nature. When the individual perceives his duty and performs it in accordance with the dictates of his soul, he paves the way for fraternal society. He emphasises, man-making is essentially a problem of becoming; theories, education, religion and things like these may assist but each individual will have to acquire his freedom—each will have to work out his own salvation. He should have a motto for the purpose which Vivekananda sumps up in just two words: renunciation and service. Man-making is another name for individual perfection and therefore the emphasis in his social theory is upon individuality.

In Vivekananda's philosophy renunciation and service are the convex and the concave surface of the same coin. Renunciation is never the end of his ethics; it is just the beginning—it is its open sesame. Renunciation culminates in loving service to fellowmen. It implies giving up attachment to small things for achieving something great. It is indeed a conquest and in its very nature requires sustained and determined effort, absorption in the work undertaken, and indifference to everything extraneous to it. By such absorption, by choosing toil and refusing ease, that Stephenson, for instance, invented the steam engine.[2] He exhorts mankind to the task of building good society by realising the eternal qualities like *freedom, equality, brotherhood*, etc. Good society depends upon the principle of right relation of the individual to society. When everyone is by instinct a seeker of happiness, the greatest welfare can be promoted if they can come to an agreement and seek the happiness of all. Thus it is enlightened self-interest or 'unadulterated common sense pure and simple' that can determine the principle of proper relation between individual and society and thereby promote happiness of man in society.

Vivekananda holds that common sense or reason alone could never be the eternal guarantee of philanthropy. He said, "Utilitarian standards cannot explain the ethical relations of men, for. . . . we cannot derive any ethical laws from consideration of utility. The utilitarian. . . . asks us to take up ethics and good to society. . . . why should I do good to other men, and not injure them? If happiness is the goal of mankind, why should I not make myself happy and others unhappy? What prevents me?".[3] To him, what is needed is a faith—a religion—in addition to reason. It is rational faith alone which can mould ideal social partnership.

Renunciation results in service or rather service is the medium in and through which renunciation manifests itself. Service is never an act of charity; it is pure, selfless act of love done to others, *prima facie* in disregard of consequences but, in ultimate analysis, for leading them to the road of freedom. *Annadana, vidyadana, jnanadana* and other acts of charity are only means for enabling the man in bondage to secure freedom. The giver himself attains freedom in the process, for thereby he perceives harmony with all things and realises his true self. Man is not a solitary animal; he lives, moves and has his being in social setting and; therefore, for fuller life he must perceive harmony with his neighbours.

Plato has a parallel concept of *renunciation*-service. He emphasises a sense of social duty, rather than a struggle for individual rights, in his quest of justice, which is synonymous with virtue and goodness. Good society, for him, rests in a stratified system of social functions, under which individual perceives his duty and performs it in accordance with the dictates of the soul. What Plato prescribes may be described as spiritualisation of social relationships which, according to Vivekananda, should be the basis of and watchword of civilisation.

According to Vivekananda, religion never consists of dogmas; religion implies "the conquering of the inner man, understanding the secrets of the subtle working that are within the human mind, and knowing its wonderful secrets". And science is, according to him, nothing other than "comprehending the laws that govern the particles of matter outside us. Thus science and religion are never antithetical in nature; they are really complementary. All knowledge is but a part of the religion and science is nothing but the finding of Unity. This act of proving the unity of science and religion is but a part of his philosophy of assimilation and synthesis. Prof. Ainslie T.E. Embree said, "At a time when some of the strongest voices in India were equating any accommodation with western ideas as an attack on the traditional religious values of India, Vivekananda argued that the science was neutral; it could enrich, not weaken Indian life".[4]

According to Marcus Aurelius, "My city and country, so far as I am Antonius is Rome, but so far as I am a man, it is the world".[5] We find an echo of this in Vivekananda when he says: "I belong to India as much as to the world". Another name of this synthetic outlook is 'the ideal of the universal man' towards which philosophers have been striving since the days of the stoics and which, according to Vivekananda, is an essential part of India's message to the world".[6] Vivekananda practically identifies the ideal with true Brahminhood. To him, the Brahmin does not represent a caste but an ideal—the ideal of spiritual values. A true or an ideal Brahmin is a man of renunciation and culture. He forsakes small things for attaining to something great. To perceive harmony with all other human beings the individual is required to broaden his cultural outlook. This is essentially an aspect of renunciation, for it signifies taking leave of all forms of chauvinism and eagerness to understand and appreciate other ways and views of life.

Self-respect is essentially a human property; it lies at the base of all religions, all missions and all forms of growth. If it is sin to lose faith in man, it is a far greater sin to lose faith in oneself. Vivekananda passionately preached its inculcation. His own life was ceaseless practices of the cult. Creed of renunciation for group life implies fearlessness which can come only out of renunciation. To be self-respecting a people, like an individual, must renounce all shades of selfishness.

Vivekananda is in complete agreement with J.S. Mill and others that with small men no great thing can really be accomplished. Liberty being the first condition of growth, what the individual requires for his perfection is all-round freedom. This led him to modify his organic conception of society a little. Although in his view, society is essentially of organic character, he never seeks to identify the will and personality of the individual with those of all. In his philosophy, society clearly exists for the growth both of the individual and of its own.

Vivekananda asserts that self-promotion must always be 'from within' and 'according to one's own law of growth' and that the 'historically acquired character of a people' must be preserved. To him, society is always under the discipline of a high purpose—the purpose of securing the growth of the individual and that of its own. It sets up the governmental agency for securing the object. If the agency becomes perverted, the social purpose should be sought to be served by ignoring the existence of the agency altogether.

REFERENCES

. *Vivekananda, The Complete Works of Swami Vivekananda,* Vol. I, Mayavati Memorial edn., Advaita Ashram, Calcutta, 1957, pp. XIV-XV.

2. *Sister Nivedita*, Aggressive Hinduism, Udbodhan, Calcutta, 1950, p. 9.
3. Vivekananda, *The Complete Works of Swami Vivekananda*, Vol. II, Mayavati Memorial edn., Advaita Ashram, Calcutta, 1958, pp. 63-64.
4. *Ibid.*, p. 519.
5. *Ibid.*, p. 612.
6. *Ibid.*, p. 664.

6

VIVEKANANDA ON RELIGION

Vivekananda considered the *Vedas* and the *Upanishads* as the source of Hindu religion and culture. Throughout his life he tried to interpret correctly the philosophy of the *Upanishads*. Apart from its religion and philosophy, he found that the *Upanishads* paved the way for the salvation of mankind. He also found that the *Upanishads* taught the solidarity of this universe-brotherhood of man. He was inspired by the *Upanishadic* call to shed all ignorance which divides us and makes us hate one another. It was as if his Master and the philosophy of the *Upanishads* conspired to shape Vivekananda's personality and philosophy which he preached throughout his short life of intense activity.

Vivekananda was also impressed by the teachings of Gautam Buddha, whose main concern was removal of sufferings of mankind. The Buddha renounced the world not for the purpose of seeking his own salvation but for finding a way out for the world burning with all kinds of miseries. He expressed his regard for the Buddha. He said, "I would like to see moral men like Gautam Buddha, who did not believe in a personal God or a personal soul, never asked about them, but was a perfect agnostic, and yet was ready to lay down his life for anyone, and worked all his life for the good of all, and thought only of the good of all".[1]

Vivekananda never claimed to be a philosopher or a social reformer in the traditional sense of the term. He was, in fact, only a religious person. He thought that if religion is interpreted in its correct sense and understood by everybody, much of our miseries, mutual conflicts and social evils would be automatically solved. He stressed the importance of religion especially in an age when the world was fast moving in its progress in the fields of science and technology. He considered religion as the healthiest exercise that the human mind could have. Religion has always worked as a great motive force but unfortunately it has also remained a basis of conflicts among mankind. Different religions have the same goal, but the paths and other details differ. It is the ritualistic domination of religions which becomes the point of conflict. He stressed on unity of all relgions, fusion of all religions.

Vivekananda tried to explain the real significance of religion. According to him, true religion must have a positive approach. It must not only teach man to refrain from evil but must insist on doing good to others. Religion must awake the spirit within men. He said, "Religion is the idea which is raising the brute unto man, and man unto God".[2] If religion is taken away from human society, the residue will be a mass of brutes. It constitutes man's very nature and unites him to his fellows; it gives vision and inspiration to him. He taught love and tolerance as the cardinal principles of religion. He preached tolerance and religious universalism as the motto for all sincere believers in God. If one religion is true, then all must be true. Hence he insisted on harmony, peace and goodwill and discarded fanaticism, rivalries and heated discussions.

The aim of all religions, Vivekananda taught, was the spiritual integration of mankind. He said, "Our minds are like vessels, and each of us tries to arrive at a realisation of God. And God is like the water that fills the vessels of different shapes. In each vessel the vision of God takes a different form. Yet he is one; he is God in every case".[3] His aim of attending the Parliament of Religions in Chicago in 1893, was to show that the apparent contradictions in different faiths were not real. It was for this Catholic approach that he won the admiration of every delegate attending the parliament.

In establishing harmony between different religions, Vivekananda thought the *Vedanta* as the most suitable philosophy. It alone could become the basis of universal religion of man. Manifesting the common ground between all the religions of the world, it harmonised all the various aspiration of man. He said, "Love everyman as your own self and not as your brother as in Christianity. Brotherhood should be superseded by universal selfhood. Not universal brotherhood, but universal selfhood is our motto".[4] The *Vedanta* serves the basis of Hinduism and therefore he dispelled all false notions and doubts about Hinduism. Hinduism considered religion as the manifestation of the divinity already in man, therefore its outlook has been most Catholic. He said, "We believe that everybody is divine, is God. Every soul is a sun covered with clouds of ignorance, the difference between soul and soul is owing to the difference in destiny of these layers of clouds. We believe that this is the conscious or unconscious basis of all religions, and that this is the explanation of the whole history of human progress either in the material, intellectual or spiritual plane".[5]

Vivekananda emphasised that unity and variety was the plan of nature and Hinduism had always reorganised it. Hinduism has always asserted that different religions have been evolving God out of the material man, and the same God has inspired all of them. To him, a universal religion could not have a location in time and space, it must be infinite. It must embrace all human beings from the lowest to the highest. It could not persecute, could not be intolerant. On the contrary it should extend hope to all men and women, and help humanity in realising its true nature-divine nature. Such a religion was Hinduism. His special emphasis on the *Vedanta* was due to its being the universal aspect of Hinduism. He did not preach the doctrines of any particular sect of Hinduism.

Vivekananda remarked that Hinduism was more than idol worship and conventional purity. To him, the identification of dogmas with religion degraded man from his divine nature to that of brutes. Only the rational and correct type of approach in all spheres of human activity could turn every man into a prophet. He called it perfect lunacy to place eatables before the image of God for ten minutes and also rebuked zealots for spending crores of rupees on building temples while the common man died of hunger. He said, "It is in love that religion exists and not in ceremony, in the pure and sincere love in the heart. Unless a man is pure in body and mind, his coming into a temple and worshipping *Shiva* is useless".[6] In preaching rational attitude in the matters of religion and in reinstating the ancient Hindu ideals, he made a most valuable contribution to the regeneration and growth of Indian culture and also laid a stable foundation for amelioration of human relations.

Although Vivekananda had unflinching faith in Hinduism, he did not take it in a narrow spirit. He denounced untouchability. He was against the cult of the kitchen and the cooking pot. He wanted everyone to perform his duties and work for the good of others. He was an advocate of the *Varna* system of the Hindus but he would like to remove the evil practices that had crept into the system. He denounced the priestly class in very strong terms because that was responsible for the social tyranny and degradation of the masses. He criticised the old orthodox view that the Brahmins were entitled to certain privileges. he stood for the equality of all classes. According to him, all men were equal and equally entitled to spiritual wisdom. He insisted on raising the status of women and the masses. He attributed the degeneration of India to their suppression. The masses must be elevated and caste must be restored to its original foundation which was based on equality and not on birth.

The view of Vivekananda was that Hindu spiritualism had to be given a new purpose. It had to shed its passivity and fatalism. Renunciation is a means to an end and not an end in itself. Ritual is a vehicle to reach God. Superstition has its roots in fear which has no place in one's relationship with God and man. He saw the necessity of lifting his fellowmen from the morass of gross superstitions and mindless rituals. His view was that dire poverty was the single factor that had stripped his countrymen of every shred of human dignity and terrorised them into unquestioned submission. His view was that religion was not for empty bellies. He was of the opinion that the workshop, the school, the farmyard and the field were as much the meeting points with God as the temple, the mosque and the church. The service of man is the worship of God.

It is true that the whole of the attention of Vivekananda was devoted to religion and spirituality, but he is also described as the father of Hindu secularism. This is due to the fact that he talked very emphatically of the concept of religious toleration in Hindu religion. In the direction of secularism, he went beyond the plea for religious toleration. He raised the status of secular matters and did not downgrade them. He is said to have observed that what India needed was not more of spirituality as she needed bread. The material demands of the poor were as important as their spiritual demands. He stood for a complete separation between religion and social laws.

Vivekananda is called a secularist because he stood for a complete separation between religion and social laws. To him, what we want is not so much spirituality as the bringing down of *Advaita* into the material world. First bread and then religion. We stuff them with too much religion when the poor fellows have been starving.

Vivekananda was secular-minded in his outlook and philosophy. Following the teaching of his *Guru*, he considered names like Hindu, Christian, etc., as the great bars to all brotherly feelings between man and man. He asked people to break them as they had lost their significance and were proving as harmful influence turning human beings into demons in this mutual intercourse. His attitude towards other religions is best expressed in his own words. He said, "I accept all religions that were in the past, and worship with them all; I worship God with everyone of them, in whatever form they worship Him. I shall go to the mosque of the Mohammedan; I shall enter the Christian's Church and kneel before the crucifix; I shall enter the Buddhistic temple where I shall take refuge in Buddha and in His law. I shall go into the forest and sit down in meditation with the Hindu, who is trying to see the Light which enlightens the heart of everyone".[7]

In the context of Indian conditions Vivekananda was particularly concerned about good relations between two great religions, Hinduism and Islam. He considered the term *Mlenchha* as a most unfortunate one. He preached love for all and said, "Love makes no distinction between man and man, between an Aryan and *Mlenchha*, between Brahmin and a Pariah, nor even between man and woman. Love makes the whole universe as one's own home".[8] He wanted to create a new order of humanity which sincerely believed in God and the brotherhood of mankind.

Vivekananda wrote to Mohammad Sarfaraz, "The truth is that *Advaitism* is the last word of religion and thought and the only position from which one can look upon all religions and sects with love. I believe it is the religion of the future enlightened humanity".[9] He wanted two religions to form a synthesis for the promotion of common good. In the same letter he wrote, "I am firmly persuaded that without the help of practical Islam, theories of Vedantism, however fine and wonderful they may be, are entirely valueless to the vast mass of mankind. We want to lead mankind to the place where there is neither the *Vedas*, nor the *Bible*, nor the *Koran*, yet this has to be done by harmonising the *Vedas*, the *Bible* and the *Koran*".[10] He wanted complete freedom for each individual to choose whatever religion he thought best.

Vivekananda's conception of universal religion was based on the belief that God manifests Himself through all living beings. He called upon the people of India to work for the welfare of humanity besides the individual professions. He always exhorted people to seek God in fellow human beings. He often used to say, if you want to find God, serve man. He expressed his desire to be born again and suffer thousands of miseries so that he could worship the only God, the sum total of all souls. This is not only the highest expression of religion but also the clearest statement of humanism. His emphasis was on practical religion. He asked people to worship and offer the poor what they offered to the image of God in the temple. He had so sensitive a heart that once he burst into tears when a disciple of Ramakrishna narrated to him the poverty of the people in general.

Vivekananda reminded his disciples of the vows of the *sanyasins*, that is, giving up everything and doing good to others. The grand idea of identifying the cause of humanity with worship of the Divine Being was given practical shape by him. He established Ramakrishna Mission in order to open a field of activity for his disciples throughout the world. He wanted his disciples to move from village to village and help the poor. To him, altruistic service was the only religion and all other ceremonial practices sheer madness. Since its establishment the Ramakrishna Mission is engaged in philanthropic activities in the fields of education and public health. The whole force of his arguments was to bring home to mankind that religion consisted of service and renunciation for service.

Vivekananda's aim was to strengthen the humanistic trend of religion which exalts man as the true abode of divinity against the orthodox religion which portrays man as a miserable sinner, or a weak and helpless being completely at the mercy of God. His unqualified emphasis on love and service reminds us of the Buddha who also asked his disciples to wander for the welfare of many. He dreamt of a Parliament of Man for the final victory of the human spirit against the dark forces of ignorance. His ultimate ideal was the elevation of man in all spheres, religious, economic and social and thus he paved the way for the future reformers and spiritual leaders.

The *Vedanta* presented the idea of spiritual oneness of the whole universe, therefore, Vivekananda thought, it could easily become the religion of the humanity. The immense reverence for all religions which the *Vedanta* taught could overcome religions and racial prejudices and eliminate mutual hatred and conflicts. He said, "It is impossible to find God outside of ourselves. Our own souls contribute all the divinity that is outside of us. We are the greatest temple".[11]

Vivekananda's aim in emphasising the Vedantic identification of man and God was to raise the dignity of man in the world. He said, "This human body is the greatest body in the universe, and a human being the greatest being. Man is higher than all animals, then all angels; none is greater than man".[12] He was not a pessimist and refused to call men sinners in spite of all the miseries and immorality in human life. The world in which we live is the best of the world and, therefore, he never advised one to abandon it. The Hindu ideal of living for hundred years was for the fulfilment of all earthly desires.

It is very difficult to understand the development of humanistic thinking in contemporary Indian thought without taking into account the influence of Vivekananda. His humanism was based on his tremendous faith in the powers of man. He tried to direct his religious philosophy to the service of India and mankind for their spiritual uplift and total emancipation from injustice, fear and evil. His voice at the end of the last century had a telling effect on the people of India; they were awakened to revolt against suppression of human rights and all kinds of political, economic and social inequalities.

REFERENCES

1. *Vivekananda, Practical Vedanta,* Advaita Ashram, Calcutta, Part IV, 1958, p. 105.
2 *Vivekananda, The Complete Works of Swami Vivekananda,* Vol. V, Mayavati Memorial edn., Advaita Ashram, Calcutta, 1964, p. 409.

3. *Vivekananda, 'Ideals of a Universal Religion'* (Selected Works, p. 180).
4. *Vivekananda, The Complete Works of Swami Vivekananda,* Vol. IV, Mayavati Memorial edn., Advaita Ashram, Calcutta, 1963, p. 122.
5. *Ibid.*, p. 356.
6. *Vivekananda, The Complete Works of Swami Vivekananda,* Vol. III, Mayavati Memorial edn., Advaita Ashram, Calcutta, 1964, p. 141.
7. *Vivekananda, The Complete Works of Swami Vivekananda,* Vol. II, Mayavati Memorial edn., Advaita Ashram, Calcutta, 1962, p. 372.
8. *Vivekananda, The Complete Works of Swami Vivekananda,* Vol. V, *op. cit.*, p. 79.
9. *Vivekananda, The Complete Works of Swami Vivekananda,* Vol. VI, Mayavati Memorial edn., Advaita Ashram, Calcutta, 1963, p. 415.
10. *Ibid.*
11. *Vivekananda, The Complete Works of Swami Vivekananda,* Vol. VI, Mayavati Memorial edn., Advaita Ashram, Calcutta, 1964, p. 59.
12. *Vivekananda, The Complete Works of Swami Vivekananda,* Vol. I, Mayavati Memorial edn., Advaita Ashram, Calcutta, 1962, p. 142.

7

VIVEKANANDA ON SOCIETY AND STATE

Swami Vivekananda did not write any political treatise or tract. His treatises and tracts are mainly on philosophy and religion in the broad sense of the terms. He has certainly a claim to a place in the global socio-political thought both for innovation of ideas and for re-assertion of ideals. He said, "A spiritual upheaval is almost always succeeded by a political unity. . . . which in its turn helps to strengthen the spiritual aspiration that brings it into being".[1] He who, therefore, heralds spiritual renaissance becomes by the logic of the process the prophet of spiritualisation of social and political behaviour too. To quote Netaji Subhas Chandra Bose, "Though the Swami never gave any political message, everyone who came into contact with him or his writings developed a spirit of patriotism and a political mentality. So far at least as Bengal is concerned, Swami Vivekananda may be regarded as the spiritual father of the modern nationalist movement".[2]

To Vivekananda, politics is a jealous mistress of uncommon variety; more than any other it stands in the way of higher pursuits of life. Besides, each nation has a theme of life which is historically acquired. The theme of English national life is politics, the theme of the Indian national life is religion. Secondly, politics was largely what now-a-days is described as Policy-Science. It is another name for the doctrine of the end justifying the means. He said, "If you ever saw. . . . that shocking sight behind the scene of acting of. . . . politicians that revelry of bribery, that robbery in broad daylight, that dance of the devil in man, which are practised on such occasions—you would be hopeless about man".[3] Thirdly, he was quite conscious that sufficient accumulation of strength is essential for its fruitful application. The basis of all systems, social or political, rests upon the goodness of man. No nation is great or good because Parliament enacts this or that, but because its men are great and good. To him, man-making is another term for liberating the individual. Thus, liberty is his key political idea.

Liberty occupies a crucial place in Vivekananda's entire philosophy. His idea of liberty is said to offer a striking instance of the well-known tendency of the Indian mind to seek hidden correspondences between things which belong to different conceptual systems. Liberty is identifiable with several other qualities including self-realisation, salvation, truth and harmony. In his philosophy internal and external freedoms are joined into one each complementing the other, and providing for full growth of the individual's personality as both a social and metaphysical creature.

Liberty in Vivekananda's socio-political thought seldom stands alone; it stands in close relationship with other eternal problems like the nature of man, the idea of the Absolute, the nature of good society, the way of right behaviour, etc. He said, "The God of heaven becomes the God in nature, and the God in nature becomes the God who is nature, and the God who is nature becomes the God within the temple of the body, and the God who is dwelling in the temple of the body at last becomes the temple itself, becomes the soul and man—and there it reaches the last words it can teach. He whom the sages have been seeking in all these places is in our hearts; the voice that you heard was right. . . . but the direction you gave to the voice was wrong. That ideal of freedom that you perceived was correct, but you projected it outside yourself, and that was your mistake. Bring it nearer and nearer, until you find that it was all the time within you, it was the self of your own self".[4]

Vivekananda extends liberty to embrace the western concept of social and political freedom. On the one hand, liberty is conceived as freedom to perceive harmony with all things, which perception is, according to *Vedanta,* salvation; on the other, it is imagined as the state of liberation from all sorts of bondage including the social and the political. It is such full freedom that alone can determine the right relation of the individual to society. In his view, liberty is that condition which enables one, an individual or a group, to make his or its own fortune. Liberty consists in the ability of shaping one's destiny according to one's own choice. In its spiritual aspect liberty is the end. All religions and all methods of work lead to the same goal. The goal is freedom. He said, "Everything that we perceive around us is struggling towards freedom, from the atom to the man, from the insentient, lifeless particle of matter to the highest existence on earth, the human soul. The whole universe is in fact the result of this struggle for freedom".[5]

If liberty is to be real there cannot be any special privileges, nor can there be any propitiation of one by another. Vivekananda said, "The idea of privilege is the bane of human life. . . . Whenever privilege is broken down, more and more light and progress come to a race. . . . The same power is in every man, the one manifesting more, the other less; the same potentiality is in everyone. Where is the claim to privilege? All knowledge is in every soul, even in the most ignorant; he has not manifested it, but, perhaps, he has not had the opportunity, the environments were not, perhaps, suitable to him. When he gets the opportunity he will manifest it. The idea that one man is born superior to another has no meaning in the *Vedanta*. . . . The work of the *Advaita*, therefore, is to break down all these privileges".[6]

Banishing all privileges from the social atmosphere Vivekananda moves a step further to the modern concept of liberty which is both social and political in its significance.

Again, he is clear that opportunities are needed for the manifestation of the potentiality of the individual. He pines for an atmosphere in which each individual will be able to realise his self *pari passu* with others. He therefore, urges the banishment of all privileges, to create all necessary conditions and to make the environment suitable in other ways, which includes the elimination of all kinds of propitiation. Propitiation implies that one's liberty is dependent upon the pleasure of another. It makes liberty of the former quite unreal. He clearly anticipates the modern view that liberty can never be real if it is dependent upon the pleasure of others.

Liberty is not only based upon equality, but it is fully identical with it. This is spiritualisation of liberty, and it is as much necessary today as it ever was, "more necessary, perhaps, than it ever was, for privilege—claiming has become tremendously intensified with the extension of knowledge. . . . Tremendous power is being acquired by the manufacture of machines and other appliances, and privilege is claimed today as it never has been claimed in the history of the world".[7] When tyranny over the soul of man is completely broken down, only one privilege remains—the privilege of serving mankind. This is the sublimated and transmuted essence of all privileges which forms the core of Vedantic liberty and Vedantic ethics.

Vivekananda makes a distinction between the laws of nature and other laws in this connection. He said, "In this world we are bound by laws and we are striving to break through these laws; we are always trying to disobey, to trample on nature. For instance, nature gives us no houses, we build them. Nature made us naked, we clothe ourselves. Man's goal is to be free, and just in so far as we are incompetent to break nature's laws we shall suffer. We only obey nature's law in order to be outlawed—beyond law".[8] He comes to recognise the necessity of some laws in social life. He said, "This life is a tremendous assertion of freedom, and this obedience to law, carried far enough, would make us simply matter—either in society, or in politics or religion. Too many laws are a sure sign of death. Whenever in any society there are too many laws, it is a sure sign that that society will soon die".[9] Yet, social life becomes impossible if there is not division of virtue and vice. Thus laws are indispensable, but too many of them can only be destructive of liberty.

Vivekananda was no utopian thinker; he was a thorough analyst of the social pattern. The interpretation of social and political system was clear to him as it ever was to any one else. Necessarily he could not but come to the conclusion that liberty of the individual in society is irrevocably wedded to that of the group. In one of his epistles he refers to liberty of thought and action as the only condition of life, of growth and well-being. He does not urge immediate action for national independence, but it cannot be gain said that he ardently desired *Hind Swaraj* and considered national independence to be an integral part of the ideal of liberty, which is the first condition of growth.

According to Vivekananda, freedom is the keynote of spiritual life. Religion consists solely ininner spiritual urges. Wherever religion is estranged or cut off from its vital spring, Spiritualism, it is degenerated into dry formalism or dull mechanised drilling, a routine affair of life. True or dynamic religion lifts us out of our ruts. It is also the function of philosophy to provide us with a spiritual rallying centre, 'a synoptic vision' as Plato loved to call it, *Samanvaya* as the Hindu thinkers put it, a philosophy which will serve as a spiritual concordant, which will free the spirit of religion from the disintegration of doubt and make the welfare of creeds and sects a thing of the past.

Vivekananda considered freedom not only for maintaining religious harmony among various religious faiths and for realising the spiritual life by the individual, but he also thought that the individual freedom was equally indispensable for the realisation of his personality in the social and economic spheres. He, therefore, wanted to make freedom as the natural possession of all individuals. He inspired that every individual must cultivate a free body, mind and spirit.

Vivekananda maintained that the individual perfects himself by acting freely and the perfect individual, in turn, perfects society. The strength and vitality of society depends on individual initiative and freedom. It is only when individual growth is obstructed, that social assistance to the individual is justified. The individual is to be assisted and not lorded over in his quest for freedom. To him, society was only a social agency and it should not encroach on individual freedom. His belief in freedom led him to advocate for the rights of individuals in society. Liberty becomes meaningless without equality of rights. His faith in the inherent individual freedom is the basis of his defence of equal rights and opportunities for all individuals to manifest their growth. His recognition of the natural rights of an individual, in fact, puts an end to all kinds of privileges in society and establishes the right to individual equality. He condemned the privileges as baneful and tyrannical. Thus, he advocated for social equality, and in this aspect he was much impressed by the western society.

Vivekananda was of the opinion that the individual freedom should not be viewed in an isolated way, and it must be studied in relation to society. In fact, his concept of individual freedom has a bearing on the problems of the individual's relationship with society. But the society should also not be allowed to encroach upon the individual freedom. He believed that it existed for the individual and not the individual for it.

The implication of social freedom is that individual freedom is closely related to social freedom. He pointed out that none deserves liberty who is not ready to give liberty. He suggested that for proper growth, society must cultivate an assimilative outlook and receive new ideal from other communities. In other words, he meant by social liberty growth-oriented social life based on individual freedom and equality.

Vivekananda believed that social uplift could be achieved by coordinating social liberty and social equality. He regarded liberty and equality not as exclusive terms but complementary to each other. Social liberty encourages and ought to encourage social equality and unity. He demanded that the society should spend more on the education of the poor than on the rich and the intelligent.

Although Vivekananda's concept of freedom was primarily spiritual, he did not ignore the social and material sides of it. To the worldly man, material life is as real as the social life. To deny material life to him is to condemn him to death. It is only man is exhausted with pleasures of life, that he comes to know the futility of the evanescent material life and will be in search of spiritual freedom. Thus, he wanted to base the organisation of society on a synthesis of material and spiritual life. In short, his concept of freedom is all-inclusive. It stands for a synthesis of the individual and social freedom, material and spiritual freedom.

Vedantic liberty has not only equality as its complement, but it is equated with equality. Liberty is the removal of all those shackles that hinder the manifestation of individual personality. The shackles remain owing to ignorance—ignorance about the real nature of man. According to *Vedantic*, this implies, superimposition of the ego-sense by the all-pervading *Maya*. Vivekananda said, "From the days of the *Upanishads*, the Buddhas, and Christs. . . . down to our present day, in the new political aspirations, and in the claims of the oppressed and the downtrodden, and of all those who find themselves bereft of privileges—comes out the one assertion of this unity and sameness. But, unfortunately, human nature has always been found asserting itself. Those who have an advantage want to keep it, and if they find an argument, however one-sided and crude, they must cling to it".[10]

Vedantic equality implies equal advantage in social life or, more precisely, equal opportunities. This is what

Vivekananda means by limiting inequality. The identity between the Vedantic and the modern idea of equality is clear in the following passage of Sister Christine's memoirs of Vivekananda. Sister Christine said, "Imperious though he was, he had something which held this quality in check—a reverence for the real nature of man. Not because he believed all men equal in the sense in which that phrase is often glibly repeated, but because in the language of his own great message, all men are potentially divine. In manifestation there are great differences. All should not have equal rights, but equal opportunities".[11]

According to Sri Aurobindo, fraternity is the greatest of all the three ideals which the revolutionary thinkers of France had as their watchwords, though till now it is only an empty word on man's lips. As a principle, fraternity implies common enjoyment of all common equipments provided by common and cooperative effort. No doubt the boundary line between emotion and principle is very thin, but in Vivekananda's Vedantic view it vanishes altogether, making a perfect union, rather a unity, of them. To him, the whole universe is a play of unity in variety and of variety in unity. This conception of unity is the first principle of *Advaita Vedanta* which enjoins, "love every man as your own self and not as your brother". Universal brotherhood is thus superseded by universal selfhood and the ideal of fraternity assumes the highest spiritual character conceivable, in which it is identified with other sociological as well as eschatalogical qualities.

Vivekananda is largely in agreement with the modern view which seems to point to those means—material, mental and perhaps spiritual too—which the individual cannot provide for himself by making use of his equal share of rights. He lands his own colour to the modern concept of fraternity. First, the means are broadly of two categories: material and spiritual—those necessary for the mind being including in the second category. Secondly, he clearly points out that the fraternal provision for common equipment should always be relative to time and place, and as the context changes, emphasis should be shifted from spiritual to material means, or otherwise. Thirdly, he has not even an iota of suggestion that the State should be the universal provider in this respect. He clearly wants society to do this. Lastly, fraternity as conceived by him has been described as a unity partly made of emotion. Fraternity is the rationalistic way of life and since Vedantic equality embraces the entire humanity, fraternity is also pan-human in character. It signifies full-fledged international cooperation.

Knowledge is the path of realisation of unity and every bit of realisation of unity eliminates conflicts and makes for fraternity. A fully enlightened person feels one with the entire humanity and, therefore, international cooperation is a part of his *Dharma* or way of life. This, for Vivekananda, is an aspect of the state of freedom. In this way unity comes into the system of his conceptual correspondences. He said, "Each must assimilate the spirit of the others and yet preserve his individuality and grow according to his own law of growth".[12]

Vivekananda clearly indicates that adequate and equal opportunities or rights in social life are indispensable for the unfoldment of the personality of each individual. This is what is called justice or freedom in society along with others. He did not frame a charter of rights. He was very much apprehensive of the illusive bondage of duties. Although the emphasis is on duties, there is definite mention, and in some cases elaboration too, of particular rights in his discourses and tracts. Apart from rights to freedom and equality, which are practically interwoven in his entire scheme of individual perfection and of consequential social growth, there is a clear recognition of the need of right to leisure, right against exploitation, etc. In a way, however, all these rights follow from the all-comprehensive right to freedom. To him, the all-comprehensive right to freedom is some sort of natural right, inherent in every man because of his potential divinity, and the other rights that issue out of it are in the nature of civil rights—rights that society is supposed to uphold and guarantee.

Vivekananda's view of rights is only partly in agreement with the modern idea. He clearly recognises at least two natural rights of some sort: right to liberty and, therefore, to equality. He further feels that other rights which are complementary to these should also be socially recognised and guaranteed. Rights to liberty and equality follow from the fundamental tanets of *Vedanta*: potential divinity of every individual and oneness of existence of the entire humanity. Realisation of these two rights in full is the purpose of social organisation. If any objection is raised to this, one has to prove that maintenance of society is an object in itself.

Vivekananda is partly in agreement with Spencer and other sociologists regarding the concept of natural rights. He endorses their view that natural rights are necessary opportunities for self-development of man in society, but he totally rejects their principle of natural selection in this context. According to him, holding the principle of natural selection as the universal remover of all social evils is but a part of the tactics of the prosperous ones. Rights and duties are not only correlative or complementary but are also interchangeable qualities of the ethical social order. Duties in a way precede rights, and not the other way round. This is in complete conformity with Indian political philosophy which harps on the theme of duties throughout and rarely makes mention of rights. Without obligations there can be no real rights, declared both Nehru and Gandhi. In modern times Vivekananda found the same high road to right order in a scheme of duties. Proper performance of right duties results in man-making; and through this alone the realisation of the ideal, which is perfection, becomes ensured.

Vivekananda had little faith in the efficacy of legal duties, nay, in any kind of codified duties. The duties of kings are clearly prescribed in law books, but they are more honoured in their breach than in their observance. Duties should always be relative to time and place. Environments change the nature of our duties, but laws are in most cases inelastic. Codified duties are therefore unreal. The object of duty is the attenuating of the lower self, so that the real higher self may shine forth. No man is to be judged by the mere nature of his duties, but all should be judged by the manner and spirit in which they perform them. Duties must be unattached. Otherwise, it may act as a bondage hindering the manifestation of individual personality. Duty, therefore, instead of being based upon ethics, should be founded upon love, and ego should be completely divorced from it. Only when these two things are accomplished one can get rid of the idea of duty which acts like the midday sun of misery scorching the very soul. Though he is of the opinion that duty-based rights have been a contributory factor to social development, he holds that such duties, being seldom sweet, cannot go far in bringing to birth the needed rights.

To Vivekananda, political organisation is the ruling apparatus of society set up by itself for the cultivation of collective values. When ruling authority is vested in the ideal Brahmin, the organisation of duties is bound to be the inseparable function of the apparatus. In his own days he was confronted with Vaishya rule all around, the most diabolical illustration of which was to be found in his own country. Even the land of liberty which had taken the vow of government by the people and for the good of the people, had produced a governmental apparatus that conduced to the acquisition of wealth by a few. Under the circumstances, he wanted society to function independently of the ruling apparatus for the restoration of the supreme collective good-duty. Government is created for realising the effectiveness of individual self-sacrifice for the good of the many and of the oneness of purpose and endeavour actuating every member of the society for the common good of the whole.

Though Vivekananda is in complete agreement with ancient Indian social philosophers that social harmony would be best secured by emphasising duties in preference to rights, there is clear reference in his works, to a number of particular rights some of which are essentially political in character. It has been further said that all these rights follow from the all-comprehensive right to freedom. Freedom of mind appears to occupy the first place. If mind is free, no shackles can bind the individual. Freedom of mind is the motif of humanism, which is the primary message of the Renaissance. Freedom of mind implies freedom of thought and action. He found the method of sublimation in the sovereign *Vedantic* education which *inter alia* teaches stern discrimination.

Vivekananda's life was a ceaseless protest against *exploitation*. Exploitation implies complete destruction of the fundamental purpose and essence of society. Although he is an idealist, he is farthest from idealising the actual. Thus he clearly discerns recurrence of perversion in every phase of the cycle of caste. He finds both the preventive and cure in the manifestation of popular sovereignty—in the subject masses, who are always the source of all political power, becoming active in political affairs. He is a prophet of optimism; he finds immediate hope in the rise of Shudrahood in the near future. Establishment of the Shudra rules means elimination of exploitation altogether.

Vivekananda, the socialist—the protagonist and prophet of a social order is based on the foundation of justice, the components of which are not only liberty, equality and fraternity but also habitual exercise of sovereign authority by the people. This is not his ideal society, for Shudrahood, according to him, implies debasement of values. Self-government is a requisite for realising the end of society. It is also essential for the preservation of society's health. The right of self-government is embedded in the philosophy of social living of Vivekananda. It is an inalienable right of the social man. If the people have the inalieneable right of self-government, they have the right to necessary endeavour and association, too, for realising the principle of self-rule. He says that the criterion is social unity. Anything that promotes unity is necessary, and anything that does not is definitely pernicious. Applying this broad principle enlightened discrimination is to be made. Means should always be as noble as the end itself.

Right of criticising the government is another indispensable political right, and so is also the right of making petition to the government. Ancient Indian political system recognised both these rights in some measure, but they fell far short in their effectiveness to make the ideal of self-government real. They did not make people conscious of their inherent power, and mainly because of this there was no attempt on their part to organise their sporadic act of criticism and petition into united positive action. Vivekananda accepts with modification the postulate of the Hindu scriptures that society steadily declines from *Satya Yuga* to *Kali Yuga*. His view is that its decay is witnessed only periodically. But more important than this is his message of human ability to set society on the right track again. This is a doctrine of social rejuvenation which finds the greatest emphasis in *Gita*.

Religion is not for the empty stomach; nor can growth be postulated for the starved. If community life stands for any value, the man in society must be assured of his daily bread. He is to be properly equipped for the purpose, and this is essentially society's responsibility. Right to be equipped for earning one's daily bread should be supplemented by right to leisure. Vivekananda did not exactly face the problem of slavery, but he confronted the institution of serfdom in his own country and the drudgery of the working people's life in the west. He pleaded for the grant of the right to leisure to all of them. The intellectual section of the people require more leisure than others. In the past, knowingly or unknowingly society gave the priest abundant leisure, and the origin of wisdom and learning is to be traced to this.

To Vivekananda, right to property is more civil than economic in its character. It is civil, because it enables the individual to realise his self; and since society is organic in character, this he does by contributing to the common good. Property rights should be there, provided, of course, there are corresponding duties of the individual. Property is an important social institution, in as much as it enables the citizen to cultivate important social virtues. He is in agreement with Aristotle but sublimates the latter's theory further by imposing the duty on the householder to cultivate the virtues. The idea behind property, according to him, is not the western motto, 'every man for himself', but every man for others. He wants property for every householder assuming that each of them should be an ideal one. This clearly follows from his *Vedanta*. Although in his conception property may be regarded as a right, the emphasis is more on duties.

Vivekananda's charter of duties has more reference to the individual than to group life. This is quite logical in view of his organic conception of society and doctrine of man-making. The individual's life is in the life of the whole, the individual's happiness is in the happiness of the whole; apart from the whole, the individual's existence is inconceivable and the worth of society is the worth of the individuals that composed it. Duty being primarily a factor in man-making, the process should commence with the individual's life.

According to Vivekananda, "Our first duty is not to hate ourselves, because to advance we must have faith in ourselves first and then in God. He who has no faith in himself can never have faith in God".[13] Translated into the language of Vedanta it means that he who does not believe in his own potential divinity does not believe in divinity at all. Another duty of the individual is to resist evil. This is also a duty towards oneself. It however appears to be a bit puzzling, because great teachers have taught us not to resist evil: they have preached non-resistance as the highest ethical ideal. He said, "We must first take care to understand whether we have the power of resistance or not. Then, having the power, if we renounce it and do not resist, we are doing a grand act of love; but if we cannot resist, and yet, at the same time, try to deceive ourselves into the belief that we are actuated by the motive of the highest love, we are doing the exact opposite. Arjuna became a coward at the sight of the mighty array against him; his love made him forget his duty towards his country and king. That is why Sri Krishna told him that he was a hypocrite".[14] The duty of resistance in its political sense means the right of rebellion.

The third duty of the individual towards himself is to forsake all inactivity. Activity always means resistance. Resist all evils, mental and physical. Unflinching allegiance to *Swadharma* in spirit and action is the next duty of the individual. One can attain *Moksha* through the proper performance of this duty alone. It is this doctrine of sublimation of *Swadharma* by Vivekananda that largely paved the way for emancipation of the spirit as an element of the Indian Renaissance. Allegiance to *Swadharma* may land the householder in a conflict with the political authority. Political obligation, as it is regarded nowadays, is part of a larger social obligation in his view. It may be pointed out here that this is the ancient Indian view too, and this is because both in the ancients and in Vivekananda the State, which in sober reality means the government, is the extraneous apparatus of society for enforcing *Dharma* or the Supreme Law. By emphasising the duty of resistance he asserts the right of rebellion. Denial of this right implies either that the maintenance of society is an object in itself or that order is the highest good.

Vivekananda lays down that after taking up his own ideal and endeavouring to realise it, the individual's duty is to encourage everyone in his own struggle to live up to his own ideal and strive at the same time to make that ideal conform to truth. Positively it means that to attain perfection, the individual is to help every member of his species that he comes across. Negatively it implies that he is to refrain from imposition of irrational alien values upon others. In his scheme one has the right of condemning others if one is prepared to take up the duty of removing evil.

Vivekananda knew that authority is the superstructure and obedience is the foundation of every organisation. Now obedience being the overall obligation, he dissects it into a number of particular duties so that it does not remain nebulous in character. The first duty of the servant of society is to have faith in the leader. The servant is a soldier; he has no right to question or doubt the decision of the general. In the second place, the servant must not grumble about the nature of duty that has fallen to his lot. To the unattached worker all duties are equally good. He urges the worker to cultivate love for making duty sweet. The householder can discharge his love-based duties only in his narrow circle to which he is confined; but the servant of society can extend it to the entire humanity, for there is no demarcated field for him. Thus he bases his philosophy of discipline upon the ultimate foundation of love.

Authority is the aggregate forces of the people, the subject-masses, stored in the ruling machinery so that they may increase and be back to the people a thousand fold in potency, and the people in their turn may spread over them the whole community for its good. Thus the ruler is the people's regent and the sovereign is the fiduciary sovereign exercising, only as a trustee, power made over by society, and that too temporarily. In Vivekananda, there is no reference to the creation of a trustee by means of a covenant; but as the source of power is the people—the subject-masses—the government can only be regarded as the trustee. In his view, political obligation should on no account be grounded either upon fear or even upon what Bryce calls imitation, which includes reverence for the *Rishis*. But to his dismay, especially in his own country, he found that the former was the case—that fear mostly, and imitation to a certain extent, accounted for political obligation. Freedom both from fear and imitation is his credo, which maybe taken as his political watchword as well.

Vivekananda clearly recognises the distinction between *Society* and *State* in different contexts. In his view, sovereignty may be described as the 'General Will', which, to borrow the language of R.M. Mac Iver, "is not so much the will of the State, as will for the State, the will to maintain it". It is an attribute of common will, made common to community of purpose. The fact is that he does never recognise in the body politic "a power of final legal adjustment of all legal issues which arise in its ambit". What he clearly recognises is the aggregate power of the people. This aggregate power, is stored in the ruling apparatus for the time being, but ultimately it is meant for dispersal. In his view power originated from the people and ultimately reverted to them; but in the meantime, when it is held in trust by the 'ruling caste', it should be exercised by associating the people with the process, and the degree of such association should be continually increased. The key to society's progress lies here.

Vivekananda grants that a government guided by a code of laws embodying the system is good. Such a government leads to the unbroken welfare of the rich and the poor, the wise and the ignorant, the king and the subjects alike. But a code of laws always lacking in elasticity, prevents the acquisition of necessary political knowledge on the part of the people. As a result, they are not capable of any concerted action; nor can they conceive of the idea of any popular right. This doctrine of social dynamism is a unique contribution of Vivekananda to the modern Indian social and political thought.

Vivekananda's plea for popular sovereignty is also reflective of his passion for democracy, for eytmologically democracy is the rule of the people. But democracy does not imply a particular mode of government alone; it has reference to a way of social life as well. Whatever may be the form of democracy, its basic principle is always equality, and liberty and other ideals follow therefrom. Social democracy means permeation of the entire social organisation by the principle of equality. He is of the opinion that powers of society concentrated whether in the hand of the priestly or the warrior or the mercantile class are meant for transfer to the subject-masses when society attain its manhood. Society however does not always attain manhood. In his view growth and progress of society are, after a certain stage, dependent upon the manifestation of rule by the people. He clearly appears to echo Rousseau and anticipate Giddings and Hearnshaw by holding that democracy as a social pattern is consistent with any form of government. His view of democracy seems to be largely coloured by the Chinese notion of the ideal.

Vivekananda's plea for the individual initiative and social equality made him a firm believer in the institution of democracy. The liberation of the masses, involved in the concept of social equality, necessitates their participation in the activities of the government. He came to believe that some form of government by the people is in the offing and pointed out with certainty that the future belongs to the masses, *Shudras*. Thus, he identified the *Shudra* rule with democracy. By *Shudra* rule, he certainly meant the rule of the masses, and not the rule of a particular section of the society. And by democracy, he meant not representative or indirect democracy, as it is current today. His was the man-making process: it inculcates faith in self-reliance and self-government; it eliminates the dependence of the individual on parliament. It brings out the latent abilities of the individual into full play to shoulder the responsibilities of government. In other words, it makes the individual ethical, social and spiritual. But the man-making process is only a means to him, and the end is the realisation of the ideal of Brahminhood, which is without laws, government and property. The Brahmin is the embodiment of self-restraint, renunciation and selfless activity.

Vivekananda viewed democracy both as a way of life and a form of government. As a government, it could not last long without a way of life. As a way of life, democracy envisages freedom, equality and brotherhood and their union. His supreme faith in the inalienability of freedom, equality and unity made him espouse democracy as a way of life. He maintained that social evolution was possible through the cyclical rule of the caste system. The cyclical caste rule provided the theory of forms of government, namely the *Brahmin*, the *Kshatriya*, the *Vaishya* and the *Shudra*. He was of the opinion that forms of government were evolutionary, and not based on individual whims and fancies. He praised the *Brahmin* rule for its accumulation of spiritual love, the *Kshatriya* for promoting science and civilisation, and the *Vaishya* for forging international contacts. He made it clear that all these forms of caste rule in course of time became degenerated and estranged from the bulk of population who constituted the main source of power in all forms of caste rule. The cyclical replacement of *Vaishya* ultimately paves the way for the rise of *Shudra*. He identified the rise of *Shudra* with democracy, and he became their votary. He pointed out that everything goes to show that some form of rule by the people, call it what you will, is coming on the boards.

Vivekananda was an ardent defender of democracy, because he was against the rule of one or the few. He strongly believed that the new order of things is for the people and by the people. He made it clear that in all forms of government the ultimate source of power is always the subject masses. The government of the people and by the people could provide an opportunity for them to uplift themselves and mould their future. He believed that democracy encouraged individual initiative and self-reliance in administering the affairs of government. From this standpoint, he criticised the party system, which is thought necessary today for forming the government. The philosophy of *Vedanta* is inconsistent with the present party system. Hence, to avert the evil effects of representative democracy and to strengthen democracy, he laid emphasis on the man-making process through education, sacred and secular.

Every society is divided into four social classes, called

the 'castes' by Vivekananda. In however, their number and power vary at different times in regard to different countries. In the first period, the supreme guiding power is in the hands of the *Brahmin*. In the second, the ruling power is the *Kshatriya*, either in the form of absolute monarchy or in that of oligarchy. Then comes the rule of the *Vaishyas* from which community power is wrested by the *Shudras*, the labouring classes, at the last phase of the cycle. The passing of power from the priestly to the warrior class and from the warrior class to the mercantile community is a recorded fact of history all over the civilised world, especially in the western countries. But the turning of the last phase of the cycle, the establishment of the *Shudras*' rule in place of that of the mercantile community is not exactly so. Although the *Shudras* far outnumber the other classes in every society, they have invariably formed the subject-masses and sometimes, as a race, the subject race. There have been ascendency and decline of races in some cases.

Vivekananda was fully conscious of the rear-guard action of the privileged classes. Apart from the recognition of caste determined by the inheritance of more or less good or bad qualities, or what is called the qualitative caste system, there is the subtle practice of enticing the talented *Shudras* from their folds into those of the higher classes. Although he has no doubt that the effectiveness of the practice will exhaust itself in the long run, he urges the rulers to meet out equal treatment to all subjects irrespective of their caste and position, whatever may be the opposition of the other higher classes, for hastening the process of social evolution. His supreme counsel is that the teleological process of political development must not be hindered in any way; the entire pattern of political behaviour must be so adjusted as to make popular freedom possible. This is freedom for political action, and not from political action. He makes a wonderful synthesis between logic and Hindu teleology and displays his burning love for democracy.

According to Vivekananda, the source of all power is always the masses of India who are a sleeping leviathan. Whenever those in power were alienated from the subject masses, they were overthrown. The power of the *Brahmanas* was overthrown when they were alienated from the masses. The *Kshatriyas* came to power as they took their stand on the strength of the masses. They also lost their power when they were alienated from the masses. The *Vaishyas* came to power because they took their stand on the strength of the masses. He declared that the *Vaishyas* would also lose their power because they were being alienated from the subject masses. He believed in the concept of popular sovereignty. His view as that the future of India was tied up with the future of the power of the *Shudras* of the country. As everybody belonged to that caste, that meant a state of castelessness and the masses as a whole will be supreme in future as against one group of people or the other.

Vivekananda's concept of revolution is interwoven. In his view, revolution is a kind of social and political jerk which rejuvenates society after a period of decadence. Thus his theory of revolution is also his doctrine of social rejuvenation. Revolution is the replacement of one ruling caste by another. The proximate cause of this change is the perversion of the former ruling caste resulting in their weakening; but the fundamental reason is the estrangement of this class from the subject-masses. Sociologically and politically, there is nothing horrifying or illogical about the idea of returning to the democratic, egalitarian state of the ancient times. If one likes to call it primitive, the word primitive then would cease to be a pejorative word. It would rather imply the ideal of democracy and egalitarianism that mankind has as the goal of its social and political journey. According to Vivekananda, it is not actually a case of reaching, but of recovery. The ideal of the new democratic, egalitarian society of his conception is one in which all will be *Brahmins*. Equality will then become a matter of course, and democratic freedom for social and political action will naturally be vested in all.

Vivekananda fully agrees with the view that "for forms of government let fools contest", but, he adds, that is true only so long as the teleological process is served. According to him, the ultimate purpose of social organisation is the realisation of true democracy which is characterised by full freedom for political action for all, without anything of discrimination or special privilege. Till the realisation of this ideal caste rule or, in modern terms, class rule, prevails. Following Aristotle's classification the four forms of rule in their purity can be described as aristocracy, royalty, plutocracy and democracy.

Vivekananda's approach to the question of the sphere of the government is very much pragmatic. This is quite natural in view of his complete awareness of the fact that government in theory is usually not the government in practice; or, in other words, perversions are more numerous than normal forms of government. Perfection of life is the goal of human social existence. The end could not have been served so long as society remained loose-knit because of absence of governmental organisation. Society becomes property organised and purposeful under royalty. He is strictly opposed to the kind of undiluted paternalism. His antagonism to unalloyed individualism knows no bounds. His sense of community is no less burning than any one else's, and he firmly believes that ideal community life can be built only on the foundation of mutual aid. He views government as the agency for organising this and envisages performance by it of all the functions that are necessary for this purpose and also for preparing the people for self-government.

Vivekananda is perfectly conscious that if liberty of the group is not preserved, ruin comes to a nation. Defence occupies the first place in this schedule. Secondly, the government is to make the loose-knit social organisation a unity by properly organising a system of duties. Thirdly, government is to maximise welfare. Fourthly, the government is to strive for the diffusion of knowledge and dispersal of power for realising the ultimate social end. Towards this ultimate end the government is to take up as a ceaseless process the function of training the people in the art of self-government, and this training is an aspect of man-making. He is both a Statist and an anti-Statist as circumstances demand. He does not believe in the minimal theory regarding the sphere of the State; but when the State becomes diabolic and thwarts the social purpose, he preaches not non-violent non-cooperation with it but non-violent assumption of functions left unperformed by it.

Vivekananda appears to have used the terms, 'race', 'people', 'nation', and 'nationality' more or less synonymously. To him, race is an ethnic group exhibiting distinctive features in its way of life. Looked at largely from this angle, the westerners, the Indians and others are a race each. But viewed strictly, these are nothing but instances of some racial conglomerations, because precisely, each racial variety should be a more coherent mass than what any of the above conglomerations suggests. Normally a few races, when bound by a number of external ties, makes a people. For instance, the Indians are a people of various more or less coherent racial groups. A people becomes a nation when it comes to be inbued with a national purpose. Thus, to him, a people with a national purpose, whether the purpose has any political significance or not, is a nation. The Indian people are a nation because they clearly exhibit such a national purpose. He does not exclude political significance altogether from his idea of nationhood.

Vivekananda does not attach much importance to descent, because he finds that races are always mixed. A common language has been in the nature of a linguistic solution and thus a factor itself in nation-building. He admired the Congress organisation because he felt if was also doing the same thing. He agrees with Renan and others that the idea of nationality is essentially spiritual in character. A nation is a portion of mankind viewed as a unit because of a perceptible spirit or purpose. He makes no attempt to specify the ideas and ideals that a nation may get in exchange from others. He is an admirer of the splendour of variety. To him, anything that is helpful in the enrichment of national life may be had from others in exchange for your own. This calls for rationalistic selection.

In Vivekananda's philosophy nationalism being a kind of super-nationalism, it is completely equated with inter-nationalism, which has been described as a kind of internationalism sublimated. The neighbourliness and the brotherhood are nationalism and internationalism in his philosophy. He never desires complete unification, for it would mean denying the teleology that he perceives in Nature. He comes not only to join hands with Mazzini but also to sublimate him. He does not proceed so much as to assert that God has set boundaries to separate nations; but he, too, discovers in each nation a mystic soul or purpose which he alternately calls national theme and national character. He sought to bring about a revolution in outlook for all peoples. He clearly demonstrates that he has moved away from the democratic savage who was most hidebound by custom and tradition.

Vivekananda steers a middle course between international *anarchism* and *internationalism* of the safeguarding variety. He rather follows a course altogether different from both of them. He had indeed the genius to harmonise the two apparently antithetical forces of nationalism and internationalism, the combined product of which is not *cosmopolitanism* either. He holds that for a true nationalist no love is greater than that of the country, and, at the same time, in himself no feeling is so intense as the desire for perfection of the entire human race. Hence, there is the problem of synthesis which he solves by sublimating the ideal of nationalism. The developments in the practical field added to his conviction. He said, "Even in politics and sociology, problems that were only national twenty years ago can no longer be solved on national grounds only. They are assuming huge proportions, gigantic shapes. They can only be solved when looked at in the broader light of international grounds. International organisations, international combinations, international laws are the cry of the day. That shows solidarity".[15]

The nationalism of Vivekananda was in the nature of spiritual imperialism. However, it is pointed out that the very idea of spiritual imperialism is a contradiction in terms. What he pleaded for was not imperialism but nationalism based on spiritualism and hence he can be considered as the father of religious and spiritual nationalism in India. He said, "Race, religion, government, all these together make the nation. The one common ground that we have is our sacred tradition, our religion. This is the only common ground and upon that we shall have to build. In Europe, political ideas form the national unity. The unity in religion, therefore, is absolutely necessary as the first condition of the future of India".

Vivekananda explained that by one religion he did not mean denominational religion like Christianity or Buddhism. He maintained that in Hindu religion there were certain common grounds and Hindu religion also admitted variation. What he meant by religion was that certain fundamentals which were common to all religions, should be accepted throughout India. He emphasised the importance of one religion in bringing about unity in these words, "We see how in Asia and specially in India, race difficulties, linguistic difficulties, national difficulties, social difficulties, all melt away before this unifying power of religion. In the case of India, it is the only basic means of work; work in any other line, without first strengthening this, would be disastrous. Therefore that first plank in the making of a future India, the first step that is to be hewn out of that rock of ages, is this unification of all religions".

Vivekananda has rightly been called the patriot-monk of India. He asked the youngmen of the country to be fearless and work for the glory of their country. He asked them as to why that forty millions of Englishmen were able to rule three hundred millions of Indians. He himself pointed out that the secret was the accumulation of will-power, coordination and bringing them all into focus. He also pointed out that the Indians lacked organisation and obedience to leadership. Organisation was the key to the understanding of the strength of modern societies and the people of India must acquire the same. He called upon the Indians to give up their slavish mentality. He said, "For the next fifty years, this alone shall be our keynote, our great Mother India. Let all other vain gods disappear for that time from our minds. This is the only God that is awake, our own race, everywhere His hands, everywhere His feet, everywhere His ears. He covers everything. All other gods are sleeping. When we have worshipped this, we shall be able to worship all the gods". He put great emphasis on national education.

Vivekananda was a great patriot and he wanted his country to be free. However, he did not openly advocate the cause of India's freedom. That was partly due to the fact that he was a monk and he did not want to get himself involved in political and legal controversies. Another reason was that he wanted to devote his whole energy to the cause of the emancipation of the poor and the downtrodden and hence he did not join politics where he would have been certainly put in prison by the British Government. Instead of talking about political freedom, he talked about strength which alone could bring political freedom. He put the greatest emphasis on strength. According to him, strength is the medicine for the world's disease. Strength is the medicine which the poor must have when tyrannised over by the rich. Strength is religion and its very essence. Strength is greater than religion and nothing is greater than strength.

Vivekananda advocated the moral foundations of national solidarity. He declared that he was an Indian and every Indian was his brother. It is true that he built his nationalism on religion but it cannot be said that he was a Communist. By religion he meant the eternal principles of moral and spiritual advancement. He believed in universal toleration and not in social and religious imposition. Besides Vedanta, his faith in international unity and brotherhood was also strengthened by his understanding of the role of science. He said, "To my mind, if modern science is proving anything again and again, it is this that we are one-mentally, spritually and physically".[16] Science is bringing the world together and accelerating universal unity. He pointed out that the old lines of demarcation and differentiation are vanishing rapidly. Hence, both his philosophy of the *Vedanta* and his understanding of science revealed to him that nations are not different from the universe. He was of the firm opinion that all individuals and nations were parts of the Universal Existence, *Brahman*. He hoped that nations by realising their individual nature would also realise the nature of universal unity. He firmly held the view that neither the *Vedanta* nor science negates the existence of different nations.

REFERENCES

1. *Vivekananda, The Complete Works of Swami Vivekananda*, Vol. VI, Mayavati Memorial edn., Advaita Ashram, Calcutta, 1956, p. 166.
2. *The Indian Struggle*, p. 35.
3. *Vivekananda, The Complete Works of Swami Vivekananda*, Vol. V, Mayavati Memorial edn., Advaita Ashram, Calcutta, 1959, p. 462.
4. *Vivekananda, The Complete Works of Swami Vivekananda*, Vol. II, Mayavati Memorial edn., Advaita Ashram, Calcutta, 1958, p. 128.
5. *Vivekananda, The Complete Works of Swami Vivekananda*, Vol. I, Mayavati Memorial edn., Advaita Ashram, Calcutta, 1957, p. 108.
6. *Ibid.*, pp. 423-24.
7. *Ibid.*, p. 432.
8. *Vivekananda, The Complete Works of Swami Vivekananda*, Vol. VI, *op. cit.*, p. 140.
9. *Vivekananda, The Complete Works of Swami Vivekananda*, Vol. V, *op. cit.*, p. 287.
10. *Vivekananda, The Complete Works of Swami Vivekananda*, Vol. I, *op. cit.*, p. 431.
11. *Reminiscences*, p. 223.
12. *Vivekananda, The Complete Works of Swami Vivekananda*, Vol. I, *op. cit.*, p. 24.

13. *Vivekananda, The Complete Works of Swami Vivekananda*, Vol. I, p. 38.
14. *Ibid.*, p. 39.
15. *Vivekananda, The Complete Works of Swami Vivekananda*, Vol. III, Mayavati Memorial edn., Advaita Ashram, Calcutta, 1960, p. 241.
16. *Vivekananda, The Complete Works of Swami Vivekananda*, Vol. I, *op. cit.*, p. 373.

8

VIVEKANANDA ON SOCIALISM

Vivekananda endorses the Marxian view that the State has not existed from all eternity. There have been societies that did without it, that had no conception of the State or State power, but he largely disagrees with the latter part of the view that at a certain stage of economic development, which was necessarily bound up with the cleavage of *society* into classes, the State became a necessity owing to this cleavage. According to Marxists, cleavage arose owing to economic development resulting in the system of private property, and the State authority was brought to birth to safeguard property relations under the cover of law. The State is thus an unethical institution. To Vivekananda, the State is both an essential and ethical institution. The ruling apparatus in the form of kingship is created by society, because unity of purpose and endeavour for the common good of the whole could not otherwise be otained. Society did not create the body politic either to ensure security or to safeguard the inalienable natural rights: to life, liberty and estates or to revive the primitive and inalienable liberty.

There is clear distinction between State and government in Vivekananda's political philosophy. During the Brahmin's rule the State was only in an embryonic form, being practically indistinguishable from society. For authority was then divided and loosely scattered. The *Brahmins* who formulated the laws and enforced them, of course, constituted the government. But while formulating laws they often gave contradictory interpretations to the scriptural rules. This stood in the way of unity of laws and of authority. By the change of governmental authority society renews its journey towards the final purpose. Therefore, his theory of governmental change is also his doctrine of social revolution and social rejuvenation.

The difficulty of presenting a clear-cut view of *socialism* is more or less three fold. In the first place, socialism implies not only a body of doctrines but a movement as well. In the second place, the doctrines are both political and economic in their import. In the third place, socialists, beginning from those who are commonly referred to as Utopians, Robert Owen, Charles Fourier and Saint Simon have always been very much opposed to one another both as regards aims and methods of socialism.

Marx is regarded as the first scientific writer. First, because he sought to keep away from *romanticism* in the enunciation of his doctrine and secondly he not only sketched the kind of society which he desired, but spoke in detail of the stages through which it must evolve. Socialist writers before him beginning from Plato down to Owen and Fourier are said to have painted Utopias, leaving disappointingly little or no guidance at all for realising these Utopias.

A *Utopia* implies an aspiration or aspirations while reality refers to fact or facts. Thus the antithesis of Utopia and reality appears to be fundamental, and because of this, two completely opposite attitudes to social and political problems are witnessed among the thinkers. The antithesis of Utopia and reality can in some way be identified with that of free will and determinism. The Utopian is a voluntarist; he, fixing his eyes on the future, thinks in terms of creative spontaneity. The realist, on the other hand, being rooted in the past, thinks in terms of *causality*. The Utopian seeks to rejuvenate the world, but he cannot do it, because he divorces himself from the process of knowing it. The realist knows the world, but as he unconditionally accepts its inexorable law, he deprives himself of the possibility of changing its face.

Marxian concept of *classless society* is clearly a Utopian element of his philosophy. Other Utopian elements are to be found in Marx's super-optimism regarding the decisive victory of the proletariat and his unlimited faith in spontaneous sociability in men. Vivekananda has the realist's approach to the problem of inequality and exploitation of man by man. Though he believes in the emergence of the perfect classless society, he does not ignore human frailty and declared that such a society will not be achieved till the moral compass of mankind is prepared through a proper system of education. Marx and Vivekananda are in agreement regarding the establishment of proletocult or *Shudra* rule. According to Vivekananda, proletocult is established when the cycle of castes is completed, and lead in this regard is given by the country where the *Shudras* are most oppressed and exploited.

According to Vivekananda, in obedience to the law of nature every society is moving towards popular rule. This is society's march towards freedom and democracy. But the pace is never uniform. Where there is regular and even transfer of power, society forges ahead; but where the making over is withheld, society is found prone to have recourse to revolution to achieve freedom. The social freedom and democracy of his conception is but another name of socialism, although he describes socialism merely as the *Shudra* rule. This view of his socialism is very much scientific, because it is in accord with a law of nature that has been historically testified.

Vivekananda is said to belong to the Utopian school, or to what is called reformistic school. B.N. Datta said, "In making an analysis of his sayings a Marxist may say that his 'Socialism' does not tally with that of Lenin and may fall short of the socialist ideal of the west; his was more of the reformistic school".[1] According to Prof. Benoy Sarkar, "Vivekananda was a socialist too. His socialism however was not Marxian". This view can be accepted *in toto* only if we interpret the word Marxian in the sense of Marxism-Leninism.

Socialism may be defined simply as *egalitarianism* and largely equated with democracy in full sense of the term. Not only modern versions like Shaw's information to the 'Intelligent Woman' that socialism means an equality of income and nothing else and Cole's assertion that socialism is a broad human movement on behalf of the bottom dog, but also old varieties like Owen's Villages of Cooperation, Fourier's Grand Hotel arrangement or organisation of society into phalanxes, Pradhon's liberal socialism, the Anarchist's dream for the realisation of the ultimate free organisation of society, the Marxian socialists' endeavour for practically the same, the Christian socialists 'Cooperativism' just to save their souls—all meet on this common ground. Socialists differ mainly because they are not agreed as to the content of equality and also as to the mode of attaining it.[2]

Equality must be associated with liberty and fraternity, which are the two other elements of a just social order. All these three can only make for unity, the index of such an order. Secondly, equality that is to obtain must be a full product, meaning that it would be political, social and economic. To put it in another way, full equality when joined with full liberty and fraternity gives us what is termed socialism. To quote G.D.H. Cole, "Socialism means four closely connected things—a human fellowship which denies and expels distinctions of class; a social system in which no one is so much richer or poorer than his neighbours as to be unable to mix with them on equal terms; the common ownership and use of all the vital instruments of production; and an obligation upon all citizens to serve one another according to their capacities".[3]

After ten years G.D.H. Cole came to inform the 'Intelligent Man' of the Post-War era that by *socialism* he meant fundamentally, a body of principles consisting, at least of the following: (1) rising standards of living, (2) personal and political freedom, (3) canons of social conduct, (4) the duty of service, (5) within wide limits the right to go one's own way, (6) adherence to simple rules of morality by members of society, (7) the brotherhood of man, (8) truth, (9) freedom of speech, (10) freedom of association for full opportunity of self-government and discovery of truth, (11) freedom of will for shaping the individual and the collective destiny, and (12) a proper system of education that can endow every member of society with right vision by teaching him truth and citizenship.[4]

According to Dr. B.N. Datta, "the reader will find that he has divided the Indians into two classes, the rich—the upper class, and the poor—the lower class. They form the toiling classes of India. Swamiji's efforts were directed in drawing the attention of the youth of the country towards the betterment of the condition of the masses. . . . Swamiji has openly called himself a 'socialist'. Therein lies the key to Swamiji's advice to the youth of his country. One will be surprised in reading that Swamiji has not only used Marx's phrase, that the poor are getting poorer and the rich are getting richer—but he has also spoken about the proletarian culture, and he has also foretold that the Proletocult. . . . of the Indian masses will be the future culture of New India".[5]

Again, "Swamiji called himself a socialist, and so far as it is known, he was the first Indian to designate himself as such. Yet his socialism is not of the same brand as of today. . . . a Marxist may say that his 'Socialism' does not tally with that of Lenin, and may fall short of the socialist ideal of the west. . . . Swamiji has denounced the exploitation of the Indian masses by the aristocrats and he has called the arguments of those who believe in keeping the masses down as 'demonical and brutal'. He said that the first step to become a patriot is to feel for the starving millions. . . . He has denounced the class-character of our civilisation, and as a remedy wanted to educate and uplift the masses on the basis of equality".[6]

Vivekananda's conception of socialism was no doubt influenced by western ideas, but its basic foundation is his *Vedanta*. The western form of socialism in the sense of *Shudra* rule or a movement for the bottom dog is, for him, half a loaf in the absence of full bread. That the masses in India were exploited had been crystal clear to him before he went to the west and saw for himself the structure of western society. By his socialism, in fact, he wanted to bring about *Yugantara*. He found in the caste system the clear translation of the principle of unity and, therefore, regarded it as socialistic. He said, "The doctrine which demands the sacrifice of individual freedom to social supremacy is called socialism, while that which advocates the cause of the individual is called individualism".[7] Socialism is both as a means to an end and as an end in itself. It is, for him, the road to perfect community life and perfect community life itself. His socialism is not a form of patriotism which has application to India alone, but it is of universal character as both a panacea and a formula of growth.

Vivekananda does not agree with any of the postulates of Marxism-Leninism. In the first place, he views history as a dialectical process, in which each period of evolutionary growth culminates in revolution, his interpretation of history can in no way be designated 'historical materialism', it can rather be called 'historical spiritualism'. His theory of the cycle of caste enables him to delineate the inexorable will ultimately result in the establishment of the *Shudra* rule. In the second place, even though he was quite aware of class-conflict, he does not think that the increasing crisis of capitalism will inevitably result in proletarian dictatorship. He believes that it is the exploitation and alienation of the masses as a whole, that will result in the overthrow of the class in power and ultimate establishment of the *Shudra* rule at the completion of the cyclical process. In the third place, the establishment of the *Shudras* rule will not bring about the desired dialectical synthesis, because not only there will be a decline in culture but something more serious may occur. He was against the principle of socialist partisanship in art, literature, philosophy and like things. In the last place, to him, religion is never the opium of the people; rather religion is the prime necessity of life, the constitutional necessity of man, and religion in some cases is the main theme of a people's life as in the case of our own.

Marx and Vivekananda are prophets of growth-oriented human freedom. According to Marx, primary hindrance is one: Private ownership in the instruments of production. Therefore, as soon as it is abolished, human beings will start functioning as self-discovering automations. Socialism is thus the way to overcome human self-alienation. According to Vivekananda, on the other hand, although hindrances are many, all issue from the single cause: ignorance or *avidya*. Owing to ignorance *Tamas* is mistaken for *Sattva*, social taboos are taken for religious principles, egocentrism is taken for the true end of life and base limitation is taken for civilisation. The march towards perfection—the growth of human life, therefore, requires the removal of ignorance which in its turn will remove all the hindrances. Marx finds the remedy against human self-alienation in socialisation of the means of production which Vivekananda finds in man-making through the diffusion of Vedantic education.

Vivekananda's socialism is not romantic in character. His emphasis is on man-making for the realisation of a perfect and just social order conceived not from an insular but the widest global outlook. Such a social order is another name for true democracy under which the mental and moral relation of man to man is organised on the highest level on the basis of mutual aid.

REFERENCES

1. B.N. Datta, *Swami Vivekananda—Patriot-Prophet*, Navabharat, Calcutta, 1954, p. x.

2. *Encyclopaedia of Social Sciences*, Vol. ix, 1944, p. 188.
3. Christopher Loyd, *Democracy and its Rivals*, *op. cit.*, p. 114.
4. *The Intelligent Man's Guide to the Post-War World*, pp. 35-36.
5. *Ibid.*, pp. VII-VIII.
6. *Ibid.*, pp. XII-XIII.
7. *Vivekananda, The Complete Works of Swami Vivekananda*, Vol. IV, Mayavati Memorial edn., Advaita Ashram, Calcutta, 1955, p. 488.

9

VIVEKANANDA ON IDEAL SOCIETY AND IDEAL STATE

Voting is a merely handy device. It is not to be identified with democracy. The class-character of the present pseudo-democratic states was patent to Vivekananda. He said, "The means is the same after all, that is, whatever only a handful of powerful men dictate, becomes the *fait accompli*; the rest of the men only follow like a flock of sheep, that's all. I have seen your Parliament, your Senate, your vote, majority, ballot; it is the same thing everywhere, my friend. The powerful men in every country are moving. Society whatever way they like, and the rest are only like a flock of sheep".[1] He goes on to say that by the system of vote and ballot the politicians rob others and fatten themselves by sucking the very life-blood of the masses.

True democracy implies organisation of mental and moral relation between man and man at the highest level, while the *Shudra* rule, though conducive to the distribution of physical comforts and ordinary education, is inimical to the growth of culture and destructive of extraordinary geniuses. Under priestly rule the foundation of the science is laid. The priests cultivate the mind, for through the mind they govern. Its demerit is that there is a tremendous exclusiveness on hereditary grounds. The *Kshatriyas'* rule is tyrannical and cruel, but is not exclusive, and during that period arts and social culture attain their height. The merchants' rule is awful in its silent crushing and blood sucking power.

The virtues of each form of government, minus its defects, when properly blended make the *ideal society* and *ideal State* of Vivekananda's conception. He said, "If it is possible to form a State in which the knowledge of the priest period, the culture of the *military*, the distributive spirit of the commercial and the ideal of equality of the last can all be kept intact, minus their evils, it will be an ideal State".[2] It will be an ideal society, because society is identified with the State in this conception of the ideal order. He is not optimistic about the realisation of the ideal in the ordinary dialectical process. The *Shudra's* rule is going to be of the same character, a class-rule, as was the rule of each of the former three castes. He is not at all prepared to surrender his ideal.

Conquer—Naturalism is the first principle of living on the part of human beings, since this is the key to their freedom. The west, by emphasising physical freedom, has gone much ahead of the East in the control of external nature. Vivekananda said, "I believe that the Hindoo faith has developed the spiritual in its devotees at the expense of the material, and I think that in the Western World the contrary is true. By uniting the materialism of the West with the spiritualism of the East, I believe much can be accomplished".[3] A perfect man is he who can work out a synthesis between his two elements—rationality and spirituality. Society being the individual writ large, an ideal society implies a perfect synthesis of materialism and spirituality.

Such an ideal society can only be imagined to be an ideal partnership for the thing aimed at by society is the realisation of the ideal of *Brahmin* of spiritual culture and renunciation in each of its members. One can naturally visualise the slow withering away of the State. Vivekananda said, "Our ideal is the Brahmin of spiritual culture and renunciation. . . . If the Brahmin is he who has killed all selfishness and who lives and works to acquire wisdom and the power of love—if a country is altogether inhabited by such Brahmins, by men who are spiritual and moral and good, is it strange to think of that country as being above and beyond all law? What police, what military are necessary to govern them?"[4]

Collaboration of classes can only be envisaged on the basis of equality. Vivekananda advocates the retention of the first-three castes, but not of the fourth, as qualitative entities during the transition period. The Brahmin will then be engaged in the dissemination of knowledge regarding the control of inner nature, the *Kshatriya* in the conquest of external nature and the *Vaishyas* in the production of material means by the application and diffusion of scientific knowledge. As regards the *Shudras*, he wants to eliminate them altogether by raising them up. He is a revivalist, because he wants to restore the caste system to its original purity. He is modern, for he is a worshipper of the authority of science. He wanted to send Indian boys for technical education to Japan, not to Europe, because though the Japanese have taken everything from the Europeans, they remain Japanese all the same.

Vivekananda is completely divorced from any kind of exclusiveness in his scheme of collaboration of classes. As a *Vedantin* he can only envisage full life, or, in Aristotle's phrase, 'good life' for all. No shadow of privilege should be allowed to enter here. There cannot be an exclusive class made up only of hewers of wood and drawers of water in the social partnership. Its foundation is duty and work, not rights and privileges. Proceeding from his Vedantic tenets he finds its easy solution in *Karma-Yoga*, the basic elements of which are renunciation and service. But he is quite conscious that *Karmayogins* are to be made, for which purpose a proper system of social education is essential. Consequently, he lays utmost emphasis upon such education. In his scheme of social education, he provides for everything that is likely to promote unity.

Harmony of classes is only the beginning, not the end. The end is the realisation of that social order which will reflect the combined virtues of all the forms of caste rule minus their defects. This is an ideal of unity in variety which postulates the fullest growth of each individual in his own line. From the metaphysical standpoint, this is the ideal of working up *Atman-Udbodhan*-making the individual free from the bondage of *avidya*. This is the function of proper Vedantic education which should first be supplemented and then by and by substitute social education.

REFERENCES

1. *Vivekananda, The Complete Works of Swami Vivekananda,* Vol. V, Mayavati Memorial edn., Advaita Ashram, Calcutta, 1959, p. 461.
2. *Vivekananda, The Complete Works of Swami Vivekananda,* Vol. VI, Mayavati Memorial edn., Advaita Ashram, Calcutta, 1956, p. 381.
3. *New Discoveries, op. cit.*, p. 166.
4. *Vivekananda, The Complete Works of Swami Vivekananda,* Vol. III, Mayavati Memorial edn., Advaita Ashram, Calcutta, 1960, p. 197.

BIBLIOGRAPHY

Adler, M.J., *The Ideas of Feedom: A Dialectical Examination of the Conception of Freedom*, Double Day, New York, 1958.

Aurobindo, *The Ideal of Karmayogin*, Sri Aurobindo Ashram, Pondicherry, 1966.

Bali, D.R., *Modern Indian Thought*, Sterling Publishing (Pvt.) Limited, New Delhi, 1984.

Basham, A.L., *Wonder That Was India*, Orient Longmans, Bombay, 1963.

Bose, S.C., *The Indian Struggle*, Thacker and Spink, Calcutta, 1948.

Brown, D.M., *Indian Political Thought from Manu to Gandhi—The White Umbrella*, University of California Press, 1959.

Burke, M.L., *Swami Vivekananda in America—New Discoveries*, Advaita Ashrama, Calcutta, 1958.

Cole, G.D.H., *An Intelligent Man's Guide to the Post-War World*, Victor Gollanez, London, 1947.

Datta, B.N., *Swami Vivekananda-Patriot-Prophet*, Navabharat, Calcutta, 1954.

Datta, K.K., *Dawn of Renascent India*, Allied Publishers, Bombay, 1964.

Dhawan, G., *The Political Philosophy of Mahatma Gandhi*, Navajivan, Ahmedabad, 1951.

Eastern and Western Admirers, *Reminiscences of Swami Vivekananda*, Advaita Ashrama, Calcutta, 1961.

Green, T.H., *Lectures on the Principles of Political Obligation*, Orient Longmans, London, 1963.

Gupta, R.C., *Great Political Thinkers (East and West)*. Lakshmi Narain Agarwal, Agra, 1986.

Hiriannya, M., *Outlines of Indian Philosophy*, Allen and Unwin, London, 1958.

Isherwood, C., *Vedanta for the Western World*, Unwin, London, 1963.

Iyengar, K.P.S., *Sri Aurobindo*, Arya Publishing House, Calcutta, 1945.

Joad, C.E.M., *Modern Political Theory*, Oxford, 1935.

Lloyd, C., *Democracy and its Rivals—An Introduction to Modern Political Theories*, Longmans, Green and Co., London, 1947.

Mac Iver, R.M., *The Modern State*, Oxford, 1926.

Mac Iver, R.M. & Page, C.H., *Society*, Macmillan, London, 1962.

Mahajan, V.D., *Modern Indian Political Thought*, S. Chand & Co. (Pvt.) Ltd., New Delhi, 1987.

Majumdar, B.B., *History of Indian Social and Political Ideas from Rammohan to Dayananda*, Bookland, Calcutta, 1967.

Majumdar, R.C., *Swami Vivekananda—A Historical Review*, General Printers and Publishers, Calcutta, 1965.

Majumdar, R.C., *Swami Vivekananda Centenary Memorial Volume*, Centenary Committee, Calcutta, 1963.

Max Muller, M., *Heritage of India*, Susil Gupta, Calcutta, 1958.

Mukherji, S.L., *The Philosophy of Man-Making*, New Central Book Agency, Calcutta, 1971.

Nehru, J., *The Discovery of India*, Calcutta, 1947.

Nehru, J., *Sri Ramakrishna and Swami Vivekananda*, Advaita Ashrama, Calcutta, 1960.

Nivedita, *Aggressive Hinduism*, Udbodhan, Calcutta, 1950.

Nivedita, *The Master as I Saw Him*, Udbodhan, Calcutta, 1959.

Nikhilananda, S., *Vivekananda—A Biography*, Ramakrishna-Vivekananda Center, New York, 1953.

Panikkar, K.M., *The Foundation of New India*, Allen and

Unwin, London, 1963.

Plato, *The Republic*, Oxford, 1921.

Prabhavananda, S., *The Spiritual Heritage of India*, Allen and Unwin, London, 1962.

Pusalkar, A.D., *Swami Vivekananda—Patriot-Saint of Modern India*, Ramakrishna Mission, Bombay, 1958.

Radhakrishnan, S., *Hindu View of Life*, Unwin, London, 1961.

Radhakrishnan, S., *An Idealist View of Life*, Unwin, London, 1961.

Ranganathananda, S., *Ramakrishna Mission—Its Ideals and Activities*, Ramakrishna Math, Madras, 1963.

Romain Rolland, M., *Life of Ramakrishna and Life of Vivekananda*, Advaita Ashrama, Calcutta, 1960.

Sarkar, B.K., *Creative India—From Mohanjodaro to the Age of Ramakrishna-Vivekananda*, Motilal Banarsidas, Lahore, 1937.

Sharma, B.S., *Swami Vivekananda—A Forgotten Chapter of His Life*, Oxford Clarendon Press, Calcutta, 1963.

Sen, A., *Notes on Bengal Renaissance*, New Age, Calcutta, 1937.

Tagore, R., *Crisis in Civilisation*, Visva-Bharati, Calcutta, 1941.

Tagore, R., *Nationalism*, Macmillan, London, 1950.

Vivekananda, S., Complete Works, Vols. I-VIII, Mayavati Memorial edn., Advaita Ashrama, Calcutta.

Vivekananda, S., My Master, Advaita Ashrama, Calcutta, 1956.

Vivekananda, S., Swami Vivekananda on India and Her Problems, Advaita Ashrama, Calcutta, 1963.

Vivekananda, S., Teachings of Swami Vivekananda, Advaita Ashrama, Almora, 1959.

Yale, Z., *What Religion is in the Words of Swami Vivekananda*, Phoenix House, London, 1962.

INDEX